Changing Patterns
of Finance in
Higher Education

SRHE and Open University Press imprint
General Editor: Heather Eggins

Titles recently published include:

Changing Patterns of Finance in Higher Education

Gareth Williams

The Society for Research into Higher Education
& Open University Press

Published by SRHE and
Open University Press
Celtic Court
22 Ballmoor
Buckingham
MK18 1XW

and
1900 Frost Road, Suite 101
Bristol, PA 19007, USA

First Published 1992

Although the report on which this book is based, was commissioned and funded
by the Department of Education and Science, the views and comments expressed
do not necessarily reflect those of the Department.

A catalogue record of this book is available from the British Library

Library of Congress Cataloging-in-Publication Data

Williams, Gareth L.
    Changing patterns of finance in higher education/Gareth
Williams.
        p.   cm.
    Includes bibliographical references and index.
    ISBN 0–335–15664–9   ISBN 0–335–15663–0 (pbk.)
    1. Universities and colleges – Great Britain – Finance.
    2. School management and organization – Great Britain.   I. Title
LB2342.2.G7W55   1992
378′.02′0941 – dc20   91–46669
                                                                CIP

Typeset by Type Study, Scarborough
Printed in Great Britain by St Edmundsbury Press,
Bury St Edmunds, Suffolk

Contents

List of Figures and Tables

List of Abbreviations

ABRC	Advisory Board for the Research Councils
CATS	Credit Accumulation and Transfer Scheme
CDP	Committee of Directors of Polytechnics
CE	Continuing Education
CLEA	Council of Local Education Authorities
CNAA	Council for National Academic Awards
CVCP	Committee of Vice Chancellors and Principals
DES	Department of Education and Science
ECS	Education Counselling Service
EHE	Enterprise in Higher Education Initiative
ESPRIT	European Strategic Programme for Research and Development in Information Technology
ETP	Engineering and Technology Programme
FTE	Full-time education
GEST	Grants for Education Support and Training
GRIST	Grant Related In-Service Training
HEFC	Higher Education Funding Council
IED	Information Engineering Directorate (of the Department of Trade and Industry)
IPR	Intellectual Property Rights
INSET	In-Service Education of Teachers
IRC	Interdisciplinary Research Centre
IT	Information Technology
JYA	Junior Year Abroad
LEA	Local Education Authority
LEATGS	Local Education Authority Training Grants Scheme
NAB	National Advisory Body (for Public Sector Higher Education)
OECD	Organisation for Economic Co-operation and Development
OST	Overseas Student Trust
PCAS	Polytechnics Central Admission System
PCFC	Polytechnics and Colleges Funding Council
PICKUP	Professional, Industrial and Commercial Updating Programme

SERC	Science and Engineering Research Council
TEED	Training, Education and Enterprise Department
TVEI	Technical Vocational Education Initiative
UCCA	Universities Central Council on Admissions
UCET	Universities Council for the Education of Teachers
UFC	Universities Funding Council
UGC	University Grants Committee

Acknowledgements

This book reports the findings of a wide-ranging study of the effects of new funding sources and mechanisms on the organizational behaviour and academic activities of universities, polytechnics and colleges. It was sponsored by the Department of Education and Science, and one of the main aims was to develop ways of assessing the effects of funding changes, based on the experiences and experiments of the 1980s; in particular the effects of the withdrawal of indiscriminate subsidy for students from overseas, the great expansion of continuing education and various government initiatives to stimulate particular innovations and to encourage increases in funding from non-government sources. The period covered by the study was one of great turbulence in higher education, and the period of calm which many in academia crave is as remote as ever. However, the period, broadly from the announcement of full cost fees for overseas students at the end of 1979 to the White Paper on *Higher Education: A New Framework* in May 1991 does have a certain coherence and logic from which it is possible to draw some more general conclusions about the effects of funding mechanisms on academic activity.

The book is concerned with the funding of institutions. Student financial support and broad policy issues such as Access, Quality and Academic Freedom are dealt with only incidentally. The aim is to see how funding mechanisms work, not to decide whether they are virtuous. However, the study does come to a number of firm conclusions in respect of such matters as institutional resource allocation, management and career development of contract staff, the pros and cons of bidding for resources and costing and pricing policies.

The research was essentially a three-stage operation. The first stage consisted of case studies of 14 universities or university colleges, 8 polytechnics and 2 other institutions of higher education. They were based largely on a series of interviews with senior academic and administrative staff and a perusal of annual reports and accounts and other management documents in each of the case study institutions. All the individuals who were interviewed have had the opportunity to react to the reports of their own interviews. The identity of the institutions taking part in the study is treated as confidential because the main aim of the study is to examine the effects of changing patterns of funding across higher education as a whole rather than to appraise particular institutions.

At the second stage nine 'theme reports' were prepared, based on the case studies. These covered:

1. Changes in general funding arrangements;
2. Overseas students;
3. Interdisciplinary Research Centres;
4. Enterprise in Higher Education Initiative;
5. Engineering and Technology Programme;
6. Continuing Education, PICKUP and INSET programmes;
7. The Alvey Programme;
8. Science parks;
9. University and polytechnic companies.

The third stage was a synthesis and analysis of these theme reports in the context of a broader review of the changes in funding to which higher education institutions have been subjected in the last 10 years or so. The book is the outcome of this third stage.

A wide-ranging study of this type is inevitably a team effort, and I wish to express my gratitude to a very large number of individuals and organizations. First thanks are due to the DES and to the Secretary of State in 1988 who saw the potential value of such a study. Although the study was overseen and greatly aided by a DES Steering Group, consisting of (at various times) Edwin Appleyard, B. Benjamin, J.S. Blake, J. Bradshaw, Gillian Beauchamp, Nigel Brown, Roger Brown, Alan Clarke, John Davies, Derek Fowlie, D. Fraser, M. Hipkins, R. Hirst, Robert Horne, H.M. Pearson, Peter Robinson, Evelyn Ryle, J. Taylor, Jim Tunley, P. van Rossum, V.R. Westlake, they are not responsible for the use I have made of their advice in this public version of the report.

Next are the 243 academic and administrative staff in the 24 case study institutions, many of whom devoted an enormous amount of time to answering patiently our extensive, sometimes probably naïve, questions.

Then there are my colleagues on the research team itself: John Mace, who had day-to-day responsibility for the first year of the study and contributed the theme report on Interdisciplinary Research Centres; Suzanne Silverman, who was full-time research officer during the first year of the study and wrote the theme report on the Engineering and Technology Programme; Cari Loder, who took over much of the responsibility for the management of the study in its later stages, contributed reports on academic companies and science parks and played a major role in assisting me in the preparation of the final draft; Janet Harland who wrote the first draft of Chapter 7 on Continuing Education; Maureen Woodhall, who is the joint author of Chapter 6 on overseas students, and George Nicholls, John Pratt, and George Delf, who undertook some of the interviews and contributed institutional and other case study reports.

Finally my thanks are due to the project secretary and administrator, Janet Harding, who has been with us throughout, and has provided an invaluable support service covering everything in the way of administrative and secretarial back-up with incredible efficiency and cheerfulness.

1
A Turbulent Decade

Rationale

Higher education is not one activity but many. Serious discussion of its finance cannot ignore its heterogeneity. Not everything that takes place under the name higher education has the same claim to resources, nor should it be financed in the same way. As Britain moves from élite to mass higher education its variety is becoming more and more apparent. Plural funding of differentiated institutions is inevitable if the full benefits of greatly expanded participation are to be achieved. This study examines the beginning of that process as universities, polytechnics and colleges moved from reliance on two dominant funding mechanisms in the early 1980s – one for universities, one for polytechnics and colleges – towards a unitary but market-oriented system by the early 1990s.

In recent years there have been profound changes in many countries in political attitudes towards public expenditure. Changes in the funding of British higher education are largely an aspect of these wider changes. They are based partly on the macro-economic view that the fiscal and monetary policies necessary to sustain high levels of public expenditure have a damaging effect on national income, and partly on the micro-economic belief that direct public subsidy of institutions is a disincentive for improvements in efficiency. Specific to higher education is the recognition that many of its benefits are enjoyed by individual graduates and their employers and the belief that there is therefore a case on both efficiency and equity grounds for households and employers meeting a significant part of the costs.

During the past decade there has been a lively concern with:

(a) the *amount* of public expenditure on higher education
(b) changing *priorities* within higher education
(c) *sources* of funds
(d) *mechanisms* of resource allocation.

This study is concerned primarily with funding mechanisms; but these need to be set in the context of availability of resources, new priorities and changing patterns of finance. Aggregate funds may be adequate for the purposes for which they are provided but users of funds will feel deprived if they consider other purposes to be more important. However, users may claim that resources are inadequate, when the real problem is that they are managed inefficiently. Conversely, providers of funds may see inefficiency when the difference is really one of values and priorities and quality criteria. Successful institutional adaptation from one funding source or mechanism to another in organizations that depend on cooperative efforts of high level professionals requires considerable managerial competence, and understanding of the issues by the professional staff affected. It is undoubtedly possible to run an organization as an academic production line, but whether such an institution would obtain either the quality or the commitment of staff neccessary for genuine intellectual endeavour is open to considerable doubt.

The heterogeneity and complexity of higher education together with distinctions between amount, mechanisms and sources of finance, between subsidy of institutions and subsidy of students, between fee subsidy and maintenance grants, and between student grants and student loans gives rise to many opportunities for confusion in any discussion of higher education funding.

Another common source of confusion is the *financial definition* of a higher education institution. This is in addition to the more widely recognized problem of the *educational* definition of what constitutes higher education. At one extreme, as in some continental European countries, the established members of the academic staff of universities are civil servants, and their salaries do not appear in university accounts. At the other end of the spectrum, in the USA institutional income and expenditure includes all capital items, all dealings in real estate, and all associated income and expenditure, such as student residences and any trading activity. There are also differences between countries in the way teaching and research are treated. In France, for example, much of the research that takes place on university campuses is funded independently of the host university and often does not appear in its accounts. Such differences of definition mean that comparisons of higher education expenditure between, for example, France and the USA will understate its volume in the former and overstate the latter in relation to Britain.

These definitional issues are important, not only because of growing interest in reliable international comparisons, but also to ensure, in a period of radical change in higher education funding, that like is being compared with like, both in comparisons over time and comparisons between institutions. There are differences between existing universities and the Polytechnics and Colleges Funding Council (PCFC) institutions; and the university of the 1990s is in several ways a different institution, undertaking a different range of activities, from its predecessor of the 1960s and 1970s.

Higher education funding during the 1980s

The period in which this study is set can be considered to have started with the announcement of the withdrawal of subsidy for students from overseas in November 1979 and to have ended with the announcement of the Government's intention to establish *A New Framework for Higher Education* in May 1991. It was a period of great turbulence, uncertainty and change, but contrary to widely held views in universities it was a decade of growth. Although it started with a 20 per cent cut in planned public expenditure (as compared with previous plans: the removal of subsidy for overseas students and the 1981 cuts in institutional support), which were the biggest reductions in income ever imposed on British higher education and reductions in real *actual* expenditure were of the order of 8 per cent, it ended with student numbers rising rapidly despite continuing financial stringency and the 5 per cent per year reduction in the number of school leavers. Full-time student numbers increased from 510,000 in 1979 to 670,000 in 1989. Of this total, 43 per cent were in polytechnics and colleges in 1979 and 50 per cent in 1989. At the same time part-time students grew from 268,000 to 396,000, accounting for 37 per cent of all students enrolled in the later year. Even the number of overseas students were at their highest ever levels by the end of the decade (71,000 in 1989). The total number of students of all kinds rose by 289,000 during the period 1979–89. This may be compared with a rise of 316,000 during the decade of most rapid expansion from 1962 to 1972. The smallest rise was in full-time student numbers in universities, which grew by only 4 per cent between 1979 and 1987 but by another 10 per cent in the following 2 years, giving 14 per cent growth in total. During the same period the number of students in polytechnics and colleges grew by 55 per cent, giving them almost exactly the same number of full-time students as universities in the latter year. The most rapid rate of increase, however, was in part-time postgraduates whose number grew by 85 per cent. Another significant feature of the 1980s was the increased proportion of women students which grew from 42 per cent of home students in 1979 to 48 per cent in 1989. Other important changes were the increase in the number of undergraduate entrants over the age of 21, from 24 per cent of the total in 1979 to 26 per cent in 1989; and the increase in the number of students attending continuing education courses (from 410,000 to 571,000 between 1980–81 and 1986–87 in universities).

One event that will never be forgotten by writers on British higher education is the substantial reduction in general recurrent funds that was announced in the 1980/81 Public Expenditure Survey. As well as bringing about a financial crisis, it was a watershed in higher education policy. No longer could expansion of core funding be taken for granted. Two useful reviews of the 1981 'cuts' and their effects are those of Pratt and Silverman for the polytechnics (1989) and Sizer (1989) for the universities.

Subsequently, for most of the period under review government higher education policy was dominated by two main concerns: to help reduce

Table 1.1   Planned recurrent expenditure on higher education (£ million)

| Year | Current prices | | (Constant 1980 prices) Deflated by: | | | | | |
| | | | RPI | | UPPI | | NI | |
	UGC/UFC	NAB/PCF	UGC/UFC	NAB/PCF	UGC/UFC	NAB/PCF	UGC/UFC	NAB/PCF
1979/80	844	571	968	655	1,113	753	1,009	682
1980/81	1,082	698	1,082	698	1,082	698	1,082	698
1981/82	1,111	748	1,009	679	1,031	695	998	672
1982/83	1,289	869	1,099	741	1,122	756	1,076	725
1983/84	1,341	916	1,090	745	1,111	759	1,063	726
1984/85	1,372	946	1,057	729	1,078	743	1,040	717
1985/86	1,399	1,001	1,029	736	1,018	728	1,003	717
1986/87	1,436	1,049	1,018	744	1,011	739	995	727
1987/88	1,593	1,146	1,080	778	1,012	729	1,051	757
1988/89	1,717	1,216	1,095	775	1,025	725	1,064	753
1989/90	1,862	1,314	1,113	785	1,038	733	1,079	762

Source: Government Expenditure Plans: Annual volumes 1980–90.

Includes government grants plus subsidized fees. Fees have been split between universities and other institutions proportionately to planned student numbers.

RPI = Retail Price Index; UPPI = University Pay and Prices Index; NI = National Income deflator.

public expenditure; and to increase efficiency by encouraging institutions to 'earn' a larger proportion of their income from both government and non-government sources, and to be explicitly accountable for it. Early in the decade the first theme was dominant; by 1990 the second had become more important. However, in 1991 the government was still insisting that although it was looking forward to considerable expansion of student numbers during the 1990s, higher education could not expect to increase its share of public expenditure.

Table 1.1 and Figure 1.1 show planned public expenditure on core funding of higher education institutions declining in real terms during the 1980s. Since student numbers continued to increase there was a fall in public expenditure per full-time education (FTE) student. This is shown in Table 1.2. The fall in unit costs was much greater in the polytechnics and colleges than in the universities because the latter restricted student numbers in order to sustain levels of expenditure that they considered essential for the maintenance of quality. Universities were able to some extent to protect the so-called 'unit of resource', or average recurrent income per student from public funds, in the early years of the 1980s because of the strong powers of the University Grants Committee (UGC) which was able to threaten financial penalties for universities that exceeded their prescribed student numbers. Until 1984 non-university institutions were subject to no such discipline and competitive pressures encouraged

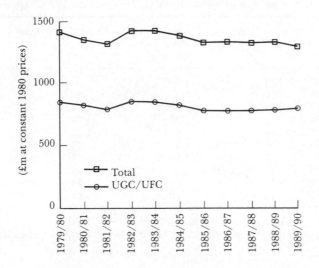

(deflated by universities' pay and prices index)

Figure 1.1 Planned public recurrent expenditure on higher education

Table 1.2 Higher education unit costs

Year	Universities (GB)	Polytechnics and colleges
1980/81	100	100
1981/82	97	97
1982/83	99	93
1983/84	100	88
1984/85	99	86
1985/86	97	83
1986/87	95	84
1987/88	98	81
1988/89	97	79
1989/90	95	–

Source: The Government's Expenditure Plans: 1990–91 to 1992–93. HMSO, Cm 1011, Cm 1511.

Table 1.3   University income by main source (£m at constant 1979/80 prices)

Year	Ex-chequer grants	Home fees	Research Council	Other Govt	OS fees	UK industry	Other	Total
1979/80	1,055	210	–	–	46	–	359	1,670
1980/81	979	206	–	–	54	–	324	1,563
1981/82	943	235	–	52	66	–	300	1,596
1982/83	1,049	131	103	47	71	23	210	1,634
1983/84	1,015	126	111	51	76	27	237	1,643
1984/85	989	124	114	54	82	37	267	1,667
1985/86	955	121	116	59	91	43	285	1,670
1986/87	963	123	128	64	100	48	324	1,750
1987/88	942	115	118	64	100	50	333	1,722
1988/89	967	117	127	66	102	55	405	1,839

Source: University Statistics Vol. 3: Finance (annual). In 1979/80, 1980/81 and 1981/2 the NA (not available) figures are included in the 'other' column. Deflated by UPPI (see Table 1.1).

them to recruit as many students as possible in order to maintain their overall income. Subsequently the National Advisory Body (for Public Sector Higher Education – NAB) and from 1989 onwards the PCFC exercised control but both were dedicated to a philosophy of expanding student numbers even if this meant a decline in average expenditure per student.

Table 1.3 shows the extent to which reductions in university regular funding were accompanied by increases in income from other sources and by other routes. At the beginning of the 1970s about three-quarters of university income came in the form of a block grant from the UGC; by the end of the 1980s the proportion was 55 per cent. This was accompanied by a 71 per cent increase in the proportion of income received in the form of grants and contracts for specific services – from 24 per cent of total recurrent income to 41 per cent. It is not possible, however, to equate specific income with non-government income since a large proportion comes from research councils and government departments in the form of research grants and contracts. In broad terms total government funds for universities remained roughly constant in real terms throughout the 1980s, while income from non-government sources, particularly income for specific research and teaching activities increased from £304 million to £662 million at constant 1980 prices, accounting for 19 per cent of the total in 1982/83 and 31 per cent in 1988/89.

Table 1.4 shows similar information for the polytechnics. Unfortunately, the statistical series are not so complete; so the table gives only a cursory indication of rather erratic trends before financial independence. At the same time as these changes in the funding sources, there were major modifications in the procedures by which basic core funds were allocated to institutions.

Table 1.4 Sources of polytechnic income 1982/83 to 1987/88 at constant 1980 prices (£m)

	1982/83	1983/84	1984/85	1985/86	1986/87	1987/88
Total income	615	557	591	656	735	900
AFE pool	434	445	450	486	532	694
Tuition fees	92	97	87	95	117	126
Short courses etc.	6	2	1	2	2	3
LEA Top-up	65	45	39	42	43	40
Research Councils	3	4	–	3	4	5
Other research	6	9	14	19	26	33
Other services etc.	9	–	–	11	12	18

Other research for 1985/86 onwards includes Manpower Services Commission (MSC) funding. AFE = Advanced Further Education.

At the beginning of the 1980s most of the income of polytechnics and colleges was obtained from the Advanced Further Education Pool. Local authorities contributed to the Pool on the basis of estimates of potential student numbers and the rateable value of industry and commerce in their area, and were able to make claims on it according to formulae based on weighted student numbers. As with all local authority expenditure much of the cash in the Pool came in practice from central government, and it was administered by Department of Education and Science (DES) officials. Cash limiting the pool in 1980 intensified competition for students since institutions and Local Education Authorities could maintain their total income only by increasing their share of the total market. The establishment of the NAB in 1983 brought some order into what was becoming a chaotic scramble for funds. It set target student numbers for institutions and subject areas, and funded them according to complex student number formulae weighted by subject and type of course. These were supplemented by special initiatives to encourage developments in particular areas such as research and continuing education.

In 1989 the NAB was superseded by the PCFC, and the centralized planning arrangements were replaced by a partly incremental, partly bidding system in which institutions were guaranteed 95 per cent of their previous year's income (against a guarantee of 95 per cent of their previous year's student numbers) but had to bid competitively for the remaining 5 per cent on the basis of numbers of additional student places and average cost of these additional places in nine separate programme areas. (An account of the operation of this bidding system is given in Pratt and Hillier, 1991.)

Changes in the mechanisms of university funding were no less radical though more evolutionary in appearance, in that until 1989 they occurred under the auspices of the UGC, and the conversion of the UGC into the Universities Funding Council (UFC) in 1989 was a much less radical reform than the parallel transformation of the NAB into the PCFC. At the beginning of the 1980s the traditional block grant system of funding universities was still in place although it had been suffering severe strains since 1974 when the quinquennial system of funding collapsed under the twin pressures of stagnant demand from students and very high levels of inflation. In 1980/81 about two-thirds of university income still came in the form of a single block grant from the UGC, and no attempt was made to indicate to universities how much of this was deemed to be for research and how much for teaching. Although there was always some degree of selectivity between institutions, details of the criteria used were kept confidential to the UGC. The justification for this secrecy was that the autonomy of universities was thereby protected. The argument was that if the UGC assumptions in making the grants were known this would prejudice the internal allocation of resources. In effect the grants were incremental in that, whatever the criteria used to calculate them, universities received their previous allocation plus an increment which was always positive, though, from 1974 onwards, always less than universities considered they needed.

The first really serious test of the robustness of these arrangements came with the publication of the 1981 Public Expenditure White Paper which announced a 15 per cent reduction in government expenditure on higher education (in real terms) during the following 3 years following an earlier 6 per cent cut which resulted from the decision in 1980 to withdraw all general subsidy in respect of students from overseas. The UGC decided to allocate the cuts on a selective basis, taking account mainly of the popularity of each university with school leavers, as reflected in the A-level scores of its entrants, and its research performance, as reflected in the amount of research council income it was earning. The outcome of its deliberations were made known to the individual universities in the notorious 'July letter' which they received on 18 July 1981. Individual universities received cuts in promised recurrent income ranging from 30 per cent to 6 per cent over a 4-year period. The UGC's secrecy about its resource allocation criteria, although intended to protect the autonomy of universities, in practice left the Committee extremely vulnerable when, for the first time in its 60-year history, it was necessary for it to impose substantial cuts in university spending and decided to do so selectively. The apparent absence of explicit criteria generated much adverse criticism, especially from universities that had done badly.

Despite dire predictions no university was forced into closure as a result of these cuts, although several London Colleges were merged and some of the smaller ones in effect closed. In part the universities were helped by a number of special initiatives which mitigated the worst effects of the cuts. Of these the largest were:

1. The 'Pym package' which replaced the former indiscriminate subsidy to overseas students with a programme of targetted subsidies (see Chapter 6).

2. The Premature Retirement Compensation Scheme which assisted the process of encouraging tenured academic staff to terminate their contracts early.
3. The Engineering and Technology Programme, which attempted to shield these national priority areas by switching funds to them.

Although all these measures bore the hallmarks of response to crisis they were the forerunners of what came to be a more systematic policy of government to steer resources according to its own strategic priorities.

Subsequent developments in UGC funding strategies focused largely on the separate identification of resources for research and for teaching. One reason was the realisation that selective funding of universities was likely to be permanent and, therefore the UGC needed a more secure basis for discriminating between institutions than it had in 1981. Another was pressure from the NAB which drew attention to the wide discrepancies between resources per student in universities and polytechnics. In 1984/85, therefore, a systematic evaluation of research activity in each subject area in each university was carried out, and this was repeated with some modifications in 1988/89. In both of these exercises a specific proportion of the UGC grant was identified as being for research. This 'R' component was divided into four parts:

1. SR or 'Staff research', intended to support the personal research of all academic staff members.
2. DR or 'Direct research', a contribution to the departmental costs of grants from research councils and charitable bodies.
3. CR or 'Contract research' which provided a small bonus for research funding from sources other than research councils or UK charities (this disappeared in 1988/90).
4. JR or 'Judgemental research', allocated on the basis of judgements about the quality of research in each departmental cost centre in each university.

Quality assessments were based largely on evaluations of publications and peer judgements. (The operation and effects of the UGC/UFC research selectivity exercises are reported in Williams, 1991.)

In 1989, following the Education Reform Act, the UGC was replaced by the Universities Funding Council (UFC) which received instructions from the Secretary of State that the Council should 'develop funding arrangements which recognise the general principle that the public funds allocated to universities are in exchange for the provision of teaching and research and should be conditional on their delivery . . . I shall expect to see . . . a means of specifying clearly what universities are expected to provide for public funds'. In following these instructions the UGC, like the PCFC which had received a similar letter, decided that something resembling an explicit contractual arrangement was necessary, specifying numbers of students in each subject area. Funding allocations were to be backed by

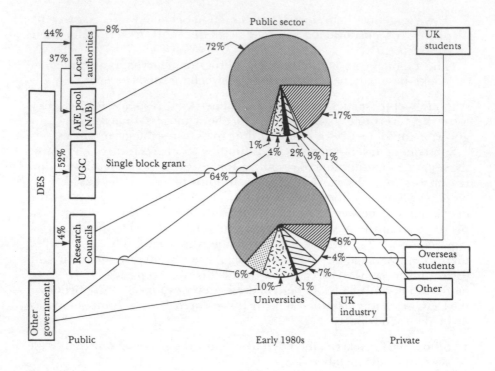

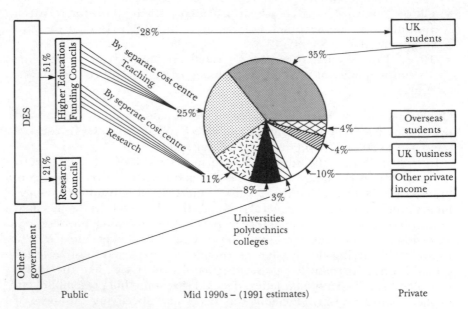

Figure 1.2 Changing patterns of finance in higher education

Table 1.5 Relative rates of growth of university income in Great Britain

	(1) Percentage change in UGC/ UFC + fee income 1981/82 to 1988/89	(2) Percentage change in Research Council 1981/82 to 1988/89	(3) Percentage change in other income 1981/82 to 1988/89	A	B	C	D
Warwick	67.94	18.40	168.37	*	*	*	*
York	66.06	40.76	70.16	*	*	*	
Oxford	51.57	10.98	53.87	*	*		
Cambridge	49.68	31.52	49.92	*	*	*	
Exeter	50.37	38.91	41.49	*	*	*	
Loughborough	59.95	56.54	32.03	*	*	*	
Lampeter	48.76	−13.16	93.05	*	*		*
Heriot-Watt	53.85	5.23	88.08	*	*		*
Southampton	55.94	−7.01	48.58	*	*		
Bath	71.34	5.75	43.41	*	*		
Sussex	49.01	−13.87	38.54	*	*		
Wales College of Medicine	47.91	−31.47	37.11	*	*		
Glasgow	45.20	32.68	126.13	*		*	*
Surrey	46.01	42.43	94.26	*		*	*
Birmingham	43.39	14.60	72.82	*			*
Strathclyde	47.66	51.74	66.04	*	*		
Lancaster	45.80	103.29	52.09	*	*		
Edinburgh	42.83	47.66	49.50		*		
Leicester	45.88	11.96	148.53	*			*
Bangor	42.78	−31.86	81.08				*
Bristol	47.50	3.78	76.38	*			*
London	45.50	−10.36	65.36	*			
Swansea	43.19	0.23	63.89	*			
Newcastle	43.87	0.10	63.60	*			
Stirling	41.90	51.50	146.16			*	*
City	39.37	58.09	85.33			*	*
Reading	42.45	73.33	68.66			*	
Kent	41.37	77.70	59.11			*	
Manchester	39.65	55.37	43.80			*	
Essex	40.71	45.62	42.93			*	
Durham	37.94	43.21	112.88			*	*
Sheffield	39.44	33.56	107.85			*	*
Liverpool	39.00	29.53	93.36			*	*
Nottingham	42.23	15.87	73.81			*	*
Umist	42.72	−5.80	49.43				
Cardiff	41.66	32.89	29.35			*	
St Andrews	29.64	89.39	160.33			*	*

continued

Table 1.5—continued

	(1) *Percentage change in UGC/ UFC + fee income 1981/82 to 1988/89*	(2) *Percentage change in Research Council 1981/82 to 1988/89*	(3) *Percentage change in other income 1981/82 to 1988/89*	A	B	C	D
Brunel	29.32	96.84	94.88			*	*
East Anglia	27.32	19.35	92.12			*	*
Leeds	36.36	5.51	87.54				*
Bradford	21.40	11.96	70.95				*
Keele	28.62	114.42	65.31			*	
Dundee	29.11	−6.12	135.35				*
Salford	17.89	−29.77	112.92				*
Hull	35.82	−32.49	95.54				*
Aberystwyth	31.30	−6.11	94.36				*
Aberdeen	25.63	−2.77	58.88				
Aston	22.10	−30.81	24.49				
Total	42.97	15.25	70.95				

2 = Percentage change in Research Council income as percentage of total recurrent income.

3 = Percentage change of other specific income as percentage of total recurrent income.

A: * = Rate of growth of UFC income is above average.

B: * = Rate of growth of UFC income is in top quartile.

C: * = Rate of growth of Research Council income is above average.

D: * = Rate of growth of other income is above average.

financial memoranda which had the effect if not the precise legal status of contracts. Subsequently in 1990 universities were invited to place bids for student numbers in each of 22 subject areas. In order to help the bidding the UGC published 'guide prices' in each subject based on estimates of previous average costs in that subject area. In the event most universities bid at the guide price for most subject areas and that particular system collapsed in the Autumn of 1990. A bidding scheme operated by the PCFC was much more successful (see Pratt, 1992).

It is misleading to consider the 1980s simply as a period of cuts in higher education resources. It was rather, as Figure 1.2 shows, one of changing patterns of finance. Overall there was some modest growth in institutional income and, in contrast to the previous decade, student numbers grew substantially. However, there were considerable changes in the sources of funds, the channels through which they became available to universities, polytechnics and colleges, the relative shares of the two sectors, and the activities for which they were used. Restructuring imposes strains on any management system. Some universities and polytechnics undoubtedly adapted to these changes much more successfully than others, and many certainly did experience a decline in the real resources available to them.

Table 1.5 shows how the fortunes of individual universities varied considerably. It ranks them in three different ways. The first column orders them according to the increase in Exchequer grant plus home student fee income, the second column ranks them according to the charge in Research Council income, and the third column ranks them according to the rate of growth of this specific income over the 1980s. Thus a university that is near the top of all three columns is one that has been relatively favourably treated by the UFC and Research Councils and which has expanded this specific income to a greater than average extent. These might be called the successes of the 1980s. At the other extreme are institutions that for one reason or another have been particularly badly hit by the changing funding arrangements of the period.

The absence of suitable published information for many of the polytechnics made it impossible to carry out this analysis for non-university institutions.

Funding agencies and mechanisms

Academic institutions obtain funds from government, households, enterprises and overseas, and they receive them through several different funding mechanisms.

Government funding depends on political priorities. Households spend according to their assessments of private benefits, their prosperity and their personal preferences. Enterprises are influenced mainly by estimates of economic returns, which include considerations of image and public responsibility. Income from overseas is largely in the form of payments for academic services and is dependent on the relative costs and benefits of buying these services in Britain compared with elsewhere. Funds can be transmitted from any funding source as a grant or in exchange for specific academic services (with, of course, a whole spectrum of intermediate positions).

Government can be divided into central government agencies with a prime responsibility for education funding, and other government agencies. During most of the 1980s the first group consisted of the UGC and the NAB. These two agencies provided 'core funds'; their grants constituted the greater part of the income of universities, polytechnics and colleges, and they had some responsibility for the economic viability of the institutions they supported. Hence finance from these sources was often described as 'hard money'. In 1989 they were replaced by the UFC and the PCFC. The new agencies, like their predecessors, receive their funding from the DES parliamentary vote. However, the 1988 Education Act and the ministerial statements that followed made it clear that their function is to provide funds in exchange for the provision of specific academic services rather than to subsidize institutions. Hence in essential respects all the public funds received by polytechnics, colleges and universities are now 'soft money', dependent on continuing satisfactory provision of specific services for which there is an economic demand. The prime concern of the funding bodies is that the institutions to which they offer contracts have the academic and administrative capability to undertake the teaching or research for which they are being paid and that there is a demand for them. This has substantial implications for the financial management of institutions.

The government White Paper of May 1991 and the November 1991 Higher and Further Education Bill herald further changes. The PCFC and the UFC are to be merged into a single new Higher Education Funding Council (HEFC), with separate councils for Scotland and Wales. But, more important in relation to the present study, the government appears to have modified its position somewhat with respect to the new councils' responsibilities for institutional funding. In justifying the retention of some elements of the dual funding system for teaching and research the White Paper comments that this: 'has the advantage of providing an overview of the public funding and financial position of individual universities, polytechnics and colleges.' This suggests that the new funding councils will have some macro-planning functions.

Until 1989, local authorities were responsible for the financial management of most polytechnics and colleges and for their core funding through the Advanced Further Education Pool. From 1983 until 1989 pool funds were allocated on the advice of NAB. Local authorities also provided additional funds; and in some institutions 'top-up' was a major supplementary source of finance. Since April 1989 local authorities have had no responsibility for major higher education institutions though they have retained some PCFC funded advanced level work in their Further Education colleges. They are, however, able to buy places for non-advanced students in PCFC institutions, and to purchase other academic services, such as research or short courses on a contract basis. By 1990, therefore, local authorities were at most supplementary purchasers of academic services. Even this will end when legislation follows the May 1991 White Paper on Further Education which proposes taking Further Education out of local authority control.

Research Councils are both core and supplementary funders. They provide the basic funding of some research centres and institutes, but as far as universities are concerned they are mainly supplementary sources of funds that have been required to meet only the direct costs of research that they fund. The maintenance of an adequate research infrastructure has been the responsibility of the UGC/UFC, which from 1986 onwards has included a component in its block grant specifically intended to contribute to the indirect costs of research council grants. This has been a frequent source of complaint by the polytechnics which receive no such contribution. However, the financial responsibilities of the Research Councils are undergoing radical change; from 1991 onwards it is envisaged that they will make a larger contribution to the indirect costs of the research activities they fund, and a significant amount of funds is being transferred to them from the UFC budget. They have also begun to accept some wider responsibilities for the maintenance of an adequate research base through the establishment of the Interdisciplinary Research Centres (see Chapter 8). Thus the Research Councils, in contrast to other funding agencies in recent years, have been moving in the direction of increased core funding responsibilities. It is possible to speculate that this role will increase in the future and that the new unified funding council will concentrate on the funding of teaching, and research closely related to the teaching function.

There are four main sources of private funding: ownership of income earning assets; endowments and donations; sale of research, consultancy and teaching services; and student fees. Sale of services has attracted much attention in recent years and has had a major effect on the management structures of higher education institutions. It is one of the main themes of the study by Williams and Loder (1992) on business funding of higher education.

The classification of student fees as a private source of income is questionable since nearly 90 per cent of the home student and 12 per cent of overseas student fees paid to British universities by students are in practice subsidized out of public funds. Obviously for the government, subsidy of student fees (and maintenance grants) is part of the public sector contribution to higher education. However, as far as higher education institutions are concerned, fee income is generated in much the same way as other private income and can be increased if more students are recruited. Fees resemble contracts in that students wish to buy a certain range of services but few students are well informed in detail about what is a satisfactory level of service; and there are very many student customers so the influence of any one of them is small.

Each type of financial flow requires different arrangements for financial management, with regard to both obtaining funds and their allocation within an institution. During the 1980s, there has been in broad terms, a shift from 'hard money' to 'soft money', away from incremental and loosely monitored formula funding by a single government agency towards more closely specified formulae and contractual funding by a wider variety of public and private funding bodies. Under the earlier arrangements the main requirement for internal resource allocation was a set of procedures for sharing a block grant amongst major programme areas and functions; and basic systems of financial audit. The procedures depended essentially on consensus, often arrived at through lengthy consultative procedures which have sometimes been described as 'collegial' in the literature.

When income is derived from many sources, and takes the form of payment for services rendered, resource allocation and financial management are more complex. Institutional management must be sufficiently flexible to respond to opportunities as they arise, but unless they are contained within a broad strategy it is easy for an academic institution to lose all sense of purpose. Broad mission statements supported by vigorous opportunistic policies and strategies, and attempts to find and exploit niches in the market are replacing the more casual planning arrangements of earlier periods. These changes have sometimes led to formal, tightly centralized bureaucratic structures in which leaders of institutions are able to marshal their whole resources very quickly: but the need to provide incentives for income generation has also given rise to universities and polytechnics as loose federations in which many management responsibilities are devolved to smaller income-earning units. Few universities or polytechnics now have time for the long, drawn-out consultative procedures which were previously a characteristic feature of higher education management in Britain.

This study explores the extent of changes in the patterns of finance, describes the responses of a variety of institutions which have had different degrees of success in obtaining income, explores the changing relationships between central management and operating units, and attempts to evaluate the new arrangements in terms of their academic and managerial effects.

2

The Effects of Funding Changes on Management Structures

The Jarratt Report

The traditional organization chart of universities and most other academic institutions was a complex diagram with an intricate network of interlocking committees, responsibilities and chains of command. The Jarratt Committee identified several features of universities that complicate their managerial and administrative procedures. They include the wide range and variety of activity undertaken; the tradition of self-government which 'can provide a strong unifying force within the institution; but it can also be used to delay or block difficult but necessary decisions'; and professional loyalties which mean that staff often regard their status as physicists, surgeons, lawyers or technicians as being at least as important as their membership of a university. This can give rise to divided loyalties and conflicts of interest. It adds to the task of uniting an institution to work to a common purpose and objectives.

The Jarratt Report went on to claim that resource allocation tended to be fragmented and uncoordinated. It drew attention to inadequate co-ordination between the committees involved in the allocation process and the fact that 'co-ordination of resource allocation relies far too much on the Vice-Chancellor and senior administrative officers and on the informal and uncertain device of cross membership of committees'. The Jarratt recommendations for a strong Central Executive authority responsible for strategic planning and the establishment of broad priorities, buttressed by devolution of detailed financial responsibilities to departments or similar cost centres was an attempt to overcome these weaknesses. The NAB report on good management practice carried a similar message to the institutions for which it was responsible. In part the present chapter is a report on how in practice universities and polytechnics have responded to recommendations, which were themselves to a considerable extent a collective response by higher education management to financial stringency and a changing economic and political climate.

Senior and middle management

Strong central leadership is now seen in many universities and polytechnics as the key to institutional success and this leadership is at least as
likely to be managerial as academic. The term 'chief executive' is
beginning to be widely used, and university Vice-Chancellors and polytechnic Directors are increasingly functioning as chief executives rather
than academic *primi inter pares*. In seven of the twenty-four institutions
that were visited during the course of the present study, new institutional
heads had been appointed within the previous 3 years and in all these
cases the term chief executive was used at least once in connection with
the post. In all cases also the appointment had been followed by marked
changes in institutional organization and attitudes towards resource
allocation. In general, these amounted to a willingness to take advantage
of the honeymoon period enjoyed by a new chief executive to bypass
elaborate and unfocused consultative procedures, to create more devolved management responsibilities with fewer levels of hierarchy and to
define management responsibilities more clearly.

In only one institution did the executive style of management of a new
principal cause serious resentment and this resulted from a failure to read
correctly the signals coming from the funding agency rather than the
management style itself. It would be fair to say that financial success is
now the main way in which institutional heads are being judged. It is not
surprising, therefore, that likely success in promoting the institution
externally and in attracting funds has become a major criterion in the
appointment of institutional heads. In several it was claimed that it is also
an important consideration in the appointment of senior academic staff at
head of department level and above.

Institutions with new chief executives were by no means the only ones
to have introduced significant management changes that were intended to
streamline management decisions. In one university, that had been
successful in terms of a variety of indicators, a senior administrator
claimed that 'we had a group of senior academic and administrative staff
who had been with the institution since it was established. When the cuts
came in the early 1980s we were determined that our life's work should
not be destroyed'. A programme that combined income generation,
restructuring, and cost reduction had been devised and successfully
implemented.

In the PCFC institutions the dominant influence on management
structures has been the acquisition of independent corporate status. In
the words of one administrator 'incorporation has created a need to
restructure, reorientate and re-equip, especially in the Finance and
Personnel Departments.' In most polytechnics the function of central
planning and institutional resource allocation is carried out by a 'Directorate' consisting of deputy directors and assistant directors with various
functional responsibilities. Most polytechnics also have a committee of

deans or heads of schools which acts as a channel of communication from individual cost centres to the directorate. There is a marked move towards the appointment of permanent deans; and managerial ability is a prime consideration in making such appointments. Four of the eight poly-technics in this study volunteered the information that deans are now effectively permanent appointments, although in two they are subject to review every 5 years.

In the universities, faculties or similar academic groupings of depart-ments, are less often used for financial management, and the position of faculty dean is generally less influential than in polytechnics. The post is almost invariably a temporary secondment of a senior member of the academic staff. The key middle managers in most universities are the heads of academic departments who are sometimes appointed to the post but are much more often elected for a fixed term from existing members of the department subject to the approval of the Vice-Chancellor and Council. The number of departments in most universities has been reduced substantially through mergers and closures in recent years. However, it is still not uncommon for a civic university to have over a hundred departmental decision making units, which along with the temporary nature of the post makes it very unlikely that, even with training, all departmental heads will be effective resource managers. This number of semi-autonomous departments also precludes the use of any assembly of departmental heads for effective institutional planning or resource allocation.

The organization of strategic planning and resource allocation

All fourteen case study universities reported the establishment of a Committee of Council and Senate along the lines suggested by Jarratt, with substantial effective resource allocation powers. In most cases this was a small committee and, it was claimed, members took pains to adopt an institutional perspective rather than protecting their own sectional interests. These joint committees were universally felt to be worthwhile. In most cases academic membership is a mixture of *ex officio* membership by institutional heads and deputies, and direct election from senates and academic boards. Council members are normally nominated by Council, often as a result of self nomination.

In addition to the joint Strategic Planning Committees, ten of the fourteen universities reported academic planning committees that ad-vised the Vice-Chancellor and senior administrators on internal resource allocation. Vice-Chancellors and Pro-Vice-Chancellors, Registrars, Sec-retaries and Finance Officers are invariably members of these planning groups. In addition, there are usually between three and six other senior academics elected by Senate. Although these academic planning committees rarely have formal constitutional status, they have considerable influence in their institutions. This derives from their direct advisory function to the Vice-Chancellor or Principal; their existence as a co-ordinated group within Senate, and a considerable amount of cross membership between this group and the more formal joint planning committee of Senate and Council. This cross-membership is undoubtedly a source of strength in most cases: however, in a few the view was expressed that there is some duplication of effort between academic planning committees and the joint committees of Council and Senate.

A second innovation in the committee structure of universities in recent years has been the emergence of influential research committees. Ten of the universities had established a research committee during the previous three years or had given much increased responsibilities to existing committees. Clearly their establishment was a direct result of the emphasis given to selective funding of research by the UGC from 1986 onwards.

Their usual functions are:

1. To advise on the selective allocation of judgemental research funds in accordance with UGC/UFC requirements.
2. To assist in the establishment of a co-ordinated institutional policy with regard to pricing of research grants and contracts.
3. To advise on such matters as publication and intellectual property rights.
4. Generally to stimulate and help promote the research activity of the university.

In two of the other universities the research selectivity function was carried out by the informal planning advisory committee.

At the time of the case studies senior management structures in the polytechnics and colleges sector were in a state of flux with new governing bodies being established. However, three of the eight case study polytechnics reported joint planning groups with similar structure and functions to those of the universities, but only two of the PCFC institutions reported a research committee along the lines of those in universities. In most, newly established polytechnic companies were expected to have substantial responsibilities with respect to the earning and allocation of externally funded research other than research council grants. Decisions about research priorities within the institution are usually a matter for the Directorate.

New administrative posts

During the 1980s most academic institutions appointed or increased the number of senior officers concerned with fund raising; business and industrial liaison; overseas students; and public relations.

All the institutions visited had expanded their finance offices during the second half of the 1980s. In the polytechnics they were enlarged and radically changed following incorporation. The additional staff are engaged partly on the improvement of financial management and partly on income generation and fund-raising. In one finance office we were told 'the traditional university finance office was concerned primarily with bean counting. The finance office in this university is now concerned more with 'financial management and income-generation than with authorizing expenditure'. This was in a university which has been successful in generating external income, but it epitomizes a general shift in emphasis in most universities and polytechnics. Finance officers have been upgraded and are now often equal in status to the registrar or university secretary.

The establishment of a *development office* concerned with fund-raising is the most recent development in many universities, but it has not yet extended to any substantial extent to PCFC institutions. Private and corporate giving to universities has a long history and many have organized appeals for specific purposes in the past. However, it has not been the practice in most British higher education institutions to have a general policy of active encouragement of endowments and benefactions. At the time of our studies most development appeals were concentrated on former graduates of the university and most of the universities were engaged in contacting former graduates or compiling address lists for future contacts. The well produced, desktop published, alumni newsletter is a feature of most universities in the 1990s.

It is premature to assess the general success of such appeals though we were quoted a few examples of six- and seven-figure donations. The amount of UK university recurrent income from 'endowments, donations and subscriptions' in 1988/89 was £48 million 1.5 per cent of the total: it had risen from £14 million or 0.9 per cent of the total at the beginning of the 1980s. The percentage figure is considerably lower than that in the USA where in 1984/85 endowment income amounted to 2.3 per cent of the much larger total income of higher education. However, there were big differences between private institutions (5.4 per cent) and public ones (0.6 per cent). As in the USA there are big differences between institutions, with Oxford receiving 5.5 per cent of its recurrent income in 1988/89 in the form of endowments, donations and subventions (followed by Nottingham with 4.0 per cent). At the other extreme are 14 universities and most polytechnics and colleges where gifts and benefactions add less than 0.5 per cent to their recurrent income.

In about one-third of the institutions visited the *industrial liaison office* had been established since 1986. In all of them it had been expanded during the late 1980s. The role and functions of industrial liaison officers are examined in detail in Williams and Loder (1992). They appear under several different names and these illuminate their functions, for example 'technology transfer officer'; 'industrial and commercial development officer' and 'earned income officer'. The term industrial liaison is used as a general term by the association of University Directors of Industrial Liaison and the Polytechnic Industrial Liaison Group. In general they are concerned with pricing policies with respect to research contracts and industrial consultancies, intellectual property rights and the promotion of links with industry and commerce.

Overseas students officers are concerned with marketing and recruitment of students from outside the UK. Members of an overseas student recruitment office often spend several weeks abroad every year in North America, South-east Asia or the Middle East. A few institutions also have close links with Scandinavian countries and contacts with them are frequent. Africa and Latin America are generally seen as less lucrative markets. In a few institutions there was also a separate European Community office with much wider functions than student recruitment. The activities of universities and polytechnics in the overseas student market are discussed in Chapter 6.

Most university and some polytechnic *public relations offices* were established in the late 1960s and early 1970s to help counteract the damaging effects of student militancy. During the 1980s their functions changed. They retain a damage limitation function in the event of adverse publicity but typically their work is now more proactive. Public relations officers had been heavily involved in the development of a corporate image in a quarter of the case studies. In marketing terms the activities of the public relations office is concerned with the general promotion of the 'image' of the institution rather than with marketing any of its specific products.

Overseas student officers are usually members of the administrative staff; frequently one of the officers in the admissions office is designated as such. The other three posts – industrial liaison, fund-raising and public relations – are divided between outside specialists and academics who have moved wholly or partly out of academic work. The balance of opinion is that public relations is a specialized function, best performed by people who already have journalistic or similar experience. In contrast some places reported unsatisfactory experiences with both former business people and former academics who were appointed as industrial liaison officers. There were, however, also several success stories where an active industrial liaison officer had generated contacts that resulted in significant income for the institution and had streamlined procedures for industrial and commercial contacts.

Experiences of fund raising development officers were also patchy. Most of those we met were former academics or academic administrators but some are professional fund raisers. Some examples of successful fund raising were quoted, usually for specific purposes, but there was a widely accepted view that Britain in the late 1980s was not a place in which many individuals or enterprises were likely to give what one described as 'something for nothing'. Whether it is cause or effect is impossible to tell but we found no institutions in which fund raising of this type has the resources devoted to it of even a modest public university in the USA.

In addition to the four officers described above which exist in almost all academic institutions fourteen had a Director of Continuing Education whose prime mission is to increase the income of the institution from short course provision. One of the roles is often to mediate an uneasy compromise between traditional adult education activities paid for largely out of general funds or government funds received specifically for this purpose, and continuing education which is expected to be self-financing and to make a profit for the university or polytechnic. This activity is discussed in Chapter 7.

Another emerging function with a specialist officer, usually a part-time academic or academic related appointment, is relations with the European Community. Most universities and polytechnics have an individual who keeps an eye on this, and four of the twenty four institutions visited had designated a specific individual with the responsibility of promoting the university or polytechnic in Brussels and keeping other members of staff informed about income earning opportunities in Europe. Several others were considering the costs and benefits of such an appointment.

The changes outlined in this chapter reflect a shift of administrative functions rather than an increase in the total amount of administration during the 1980s. The percentage of total recurrent income of universities attributed to central administration was 5.7 per cent in 1981/82 and exactly the same in 1988/89. However, within individual universities (excluding Oxford and Cambridge) the figure varied between 3.9 per cent and 8.1 per cent. A different indicator in polytechnics is that salaries of non-teaching staff were 16.4 per cent of total recurrent expenditure in 1984/85 and 16.1 per cent in 1987/88.

3

Internal Allocation of Core Funds

Models of resource allocation

During the 1980s there was a significant shift from undifferentiated block grants to institutions, to a much greater variety of funding sources and mechanisms. This helped to bring about a shift from administrative allocation and regulation towards more varied systems of institutional resource allocation and financial management, involving priorities, incentives, levies, detailed management information, cost analysis and conscious pricing policies.

Administratively a higher education institution consists essentially of a central bureaucracy, a number of centrally provided services and a varied collection of more or less specialized operating units consisting of faculties, departments and research centres. Even this simplified structure allows for eight distinct internal resource allocation procedures:

1. All income goes to the centre and expenditure decisions, both strategic and operational are taken there.
2. Income is received, strategic priorities are established and some operational decisions, usually those that have long-term implications such as recruitment of staff, are taken centrally; but routine expenditure decisions are taken in the operating units.
3. Income received centrally is 'top-sliced' for central services, and the remainder is allocated to departments or faculties which operate as semi-autonomous budget centres.
4. Income is received at the centre but most of it is passed on to departments or faculties which 'buy' services from central service units.
5. Earmarked grants are top sliced at the centre and then allocated according to the contractual arrangements under which they were provided.
6. Income earned by the operating units for the provision of specific services is retained at the centre which administers it on behalf of departments according to detailed institution-wide regulations.
7. Income earned by the operating units is subjected to a levy to cover

central costs and the remainder is retained by the budget centres which earned it.
8. All income earned by operating units is retained and all central administration and services are 'bought' as they are needed.

In practice, of course, resource allocation procedures are a mix of more than one model but broadly the pre-1980 forms of funding were consistent with the first four models while the more varied funding mechanisms that have developed since 1980 have encouraged the adoption of models 5 to 8. Academic institutions of the 1990s have multiple sources of income and resource allocation procedures usually vary according to the source of the income and the mechanism by which it is received. For example, most institutions have financial management arrangements for external research income that are different from those for UFC and PCFC income.

Thus the models can be seen as points on a spectrum. At one extreme all resources – staff, space and consumables – are allocated centrally. At the other, faculties, schools or departments are autonomous budget centres meeting their own requirements for staff, space, consumables and administrative services from income that they themselves generate and control. A university of polytechnic resource allocation system can be visualized as occupying a space that is located somewhere between the two extremes according to the percentage of its income that is allocated according to each of the allocation models. A weighted average of each item of income would indicate the degree of financial devolution of that institution.

Until the 1980s, paradoxically in a profession which placed so much emphasis on individual autonomy and academic freedom, most resource decisions were taken centrally. Four factors contributed to this concentration of financial power:

1. The most important was that allocations from the UGC and the Advanced Further Education Pool reinforced central institutional authority. Core resources were allocated to the institution, and this gave its central management the dominant influence on their internal allocation.
2. When resources were relatively plentiful few hard resource choices had to be made at the institutional level; thus there was little reason for faculty deans and heads of departments to seek to control budgets.
3. This meant that there was little institutional interference with individual and small-group academic judgements: indeed to many academics it was a distinct advantage not to have to worry about money but to know that equipment and facilities would be available if a reasonable case could be made.
4. Funding was on a long-term basis, which made it possible for strategic choices, and often more detailed resource allocation decisions as well, to involve widespread consultation and participation, at least amongst senior members of the academic community.

While one advantage of these arrangements was that middle managers could concentrate on academic leadership and not be distracted with problems of resource management, it could be wasteful on cost-effectiveness criteria. Heads of departments used a variety of political and administrative stratagems to secure staff, space and equipment but careful weighing of alternative resource use was rarely among them. There was little incentive to compare costs and benefits. One indicator of a successful head of department was to extract as much as possible of everything from the central administration. Although many senior academic staff in the universities had some experience of managing research funds there was considerable overlap between resources for teaching and institutionally determined research, and those for specific research programmes, so the financial management of a research project was usually not very demanding. Indeed, the dual funding system of the UGC was to some extent intended to blur the boundary because until the 1980s it was generally believed that good teaching and good research were inseparable.

The mechanisms by which higher education institutions receive their funding have a powerful influence on their internal resource allocation mechanisms. When a large proportion of an institution's income is undifferentiated core funding, the main resource allocation decision is how to allocate this income in accordance with institutional priorities. When, however, a large part of the income of the institution comes directly from the earnings of subsidiary cost centres an equally important consideration is to provide suitable incentives for income generation while maintaining the academic integrity of the institution as a whole. The post-Jarratt and post-corporate status orthodoxy is based on the belief that financial devolution to departmental cost centres will encourage awareness of opportunity costs used and provide incentives for income generation.

This assumes that the dominant loyalty of academics is to their subject-based academic departments and that efforts will be made for the department which would not be made for the institution as a whole. The Jarratt model can be seen as an attempt to reconcile conflicts between departmental and institutional loyalties by devolving detailed decisions to the lowest possible managerial unit while retaining strategic planning and resource allocation decisions at the centre. It requires a high degree of managerial effort and competence at departmental level. An alternative approach which underlies the resource allocation procedures of a minority of the institutions we visited is the active encouragement of corporate loyalty to the institution as a whole. In one generally successful medium-sized university this is pursued through good internal systems of communication, close involvement of the central administration with all aspects of institutional affairs and by ensuring that both departments and individuals are suitably rewarded for activities that further the interests of the whole institution. If successful such a centralized administration can enable the university or polytechnic to harness the whole of its resources very rapidly to meet opportunities as they arise.

Allocation formulae and procedures

Radical changes were being made in the financial relations between central institutional management and departments and similar cost centres in nearly all the institutions surveyed. A typical, if sophisticated, example of thinking that was widespread is the report of a working party in one of the polytechnics visited:

Existing resource allocation:

(a) Is a 'top-down' rather than a 'bottom-up' system which gives rise to feelings that:
 – decisions are arbitrary and/or wrong and are insensitive to local conditions;
 – decisions are arrived at slowly and by indeterminate means;
 – decisions are not quickly or efficiently enough translated into action;
 – decisions are 'theirs' and not 'ours' with a consequent loss of creativity/incentive to change;
 – the process is adversarial and thus, potentially, conflictual;
 – local managers refer difficult/intractable matters up for resolution.

(b) There is little apparent relationship in financial terms between 'earning' and 'receiving'.

(c) There is a feeling of powerlessness since little effective control over spending can be achieved and 'central' departments/services are unresponsive to clients' needs.

(d) Even as a 'top-down' system ours is technically inefficient in terms of (a) Management Information Support Systems and (b) the ability to critically evaluate the performance of the component parts of the institution.

(e) It is, increasingly, out of step with other (internal) systems and with practice in other organizations.

This position has arisen for a variety of reasons, e.g. our previous inability to create reserves/run deficits, reductions in our base funding, the considerable reliance of turnover variance as a prime instrument, the tight and non-negotiable calendars imposed by external agencies, confusion surrounding our management control systems, the absence of an integrated accounting system.

Many of these barriers have been removed by incorporation and our own restructuring.

The report goes on to claim that devolution should:

enhance the performance of the organisation in achieving its stated objectives by focusing the central office's attention on strategic concerns and away from day to day administrative detail.

Departmental control of day-to-day financial management should also:

make decision-making more effective through (i) a reduction in the amount of information required by decision-makers and (ii) ensuring that operational decision-takers are close to the day to day management issues and thus privy to the data required to assess alternative actions.

As an organisation increases in size and complexity the amount of information required by the central decision-maker becomes extremely large and the increasing distance from the operational unit reduces the centre's ability to assess the 'quality' of the information which it does receive. Furthermore, as the transmission of the data is likely to be at best filtered and at worst modified, at each hierarchical level, the centre will be faced with a distorted data set upon which to base its decisions.

The report also highlights some of the problems of applying general management theories of devolution to higher education institutions:

(a) the lack of clearly defined corporate objectives, testable against outcomes, which could be used to assess Departmental performance; (In such circumstances localized managerial discretion may not increase institutional efficiency in the allocation of resources.)

(b) the hierarchical level at which devolution ought to operate is much less clear in Higher Education; (It could be argued that incentives would be maximized and transaction costs minimized if the Polytechnic were to devolve to courses as cost centres.)

(c) the identification of 'essential' central services, i.e. those for which Departments would be charged regardless of the use they make of them; (These constitute public goods which are held to be central to the achievement of corporate objectives but, in so far as the differential use made of them by Departments is not reflected in differential payments, their funding is problematic. Further, incentives to efficiency improvements are reduced by such central services not being able to demonstrate their competitive ability.)

(d) in a not-for-profit institution surpluses cannot readily be distributed but losses will attract penalties to decision-makers;

(e) the Polytechnic's outputs are produced by cooperative teams to which the application of personal incentive schemes is highly problematic;

(f) inter-Departmental trading would result in transaction costs surrounding the negotiation and policing of contracts and, in the presence of alternative sources of supply, increase the possibility of trade wars; (Administered prices would reduce this possibility but at the costs of reduced efficiency gains.)

(g) the operation of such a devolved approach would be dependent upon central decision-makers being prepared to operate a 'hands-off' approach despite the temptation to intervene. Actual or expected central intervention would reduce the Department's incentives to aim for efficiency savings and would raise expectations that budgetary shortfalls, at Departmental level, would be made good by the centre.

Three other fundamental criticisms of financial devolution are often made. One is that leading academics often do not possess the necessary management skills and financial devolution has not always been accompanied by appropriate training and administrative back-up. The second is that it is inappropriate for senior academic staff to spend a large proportion of their time on financial management. The third is that management information systems are inadequate for most academic departments to take full financial responsibility for their affairs.

It is generally accepted that a financially autonomous budget centre must be of a certain minimum size but there is no accepted view about what that size is. Figures are quoted ranging from 10 to 50 academic staff as the minimum size a unit needs to be before it can be expected to undertake the responsibility of financial self management. One of the reasons for the confusion is that devolution has a variety of different meanings with big differences between institutions in:

(a) the formulae or other procedures by which departmental allocations are determined;
(b) the budget heads over which the department has control;
(c) the extent of virement between budget heads;
(d) the possibility of carrying forward surpluses or deficits.

The following paragraphs describe the basic systems of resource allocation in the case study universities in these terms.

University resource allocation procedures

Of the fourteen case study universities, four had budgets that were devolved entirely to departmental or similar cost centres. This included responsibility for academic staff salaries but not payments for the use of space or for central administrative services. In addition, one large civic university has devolved full financial responsibilities (other than central services) to twelve spending units which correspond broadly to faculties consisting of groups of departments in related subject areas. Of the remainder, three reported that all current expenditure other than academic salaries was now devolved to departments, four reported partial devolution and three claimed, in the words of one respondent, 'not to have gone far down the road of devolved financial responsibilities to departments'.

In the universities that have moved or were moving towards substantial financial devolution, two principal reasons were given: implementation of Jarratt recommendations and the need for departments to be properly informed about their share of any projected shortfall in institutional funds, and the contribution they should be making to overcoming it. (Jarratt was also mentioned as an indirect influence in two non-university institutions.) In all but one of the universities with fully devolved budgets, the departmental target was a target for *savings*. This, at least, partly justifies the view, expressed on two occasions in centralized institutions, that financial devolution sometimes reflects an abdication by institutional managers of their responsibility to implement university decisions about academic priorities.

Two of the universities, without significant financial devolution to departments, reported that the basis of financial allocation within the university was largely historical. Cost centres receive staff, space and other resources on an incremental basis. In contrast, another, also with limited financial devolution, has an annual zero based budgeting procedure, rather similar to the Public Expenditure Survey Committee. A small committee of senior administrators and academics evaluates departmental bids in the light of previous performance, the UFC allocation criteria and the university's 5-year rolling plan. A provisional allocation is discussed with each departmental head individually but once the final allocation is made the department must adhere to it and only limited virement is possible between subject heads and surpluses cannot be carried forward. This system is atypical but it is reported because its supporters claim that it has proved itself to be robust at a time of financial stringency as well as in the period of expansion in which it was first established. It is acknowledged that the procedure is time consuming: central administrative expenditures as a percentage of total expenditure are above average in this university, though at 6.1 per cent not exorbitantly so. However, apart from the resource allocation functions, the annual interviews with departmental chairmen serve the useful purpose of departmental review, and keep central administrators well informed about the work of each department.

In the other eleven universities some form of formula allocation to departments was reported. In most cases the formulae are based on student numbers: in a few income generation is rewarded directly through the departmental formula, although it is more usual for this to be included in the distribution of earned income which is discussed in the next chapter. It is very rare for a university to use UFC research ratings explicitly as a basis for selective allocation of funds to departments. While most take external research ratings into consideration, almost all claim that the greater part of the allocation is on the basis of institutional judgements and formulae which take independent account of publications, research grant income, PhD completions and, in one case, independent evaluations of research performance.

Three examples of formulae allocation in universities are shown in Tables 3.1–3.3.

The essence of another formula in a university with complete financial devolution to departments is that, after top slicing of 30 per cent for central

Table 3.1   Departmental formula for departmental allocations: in university A

The main principles of the formula are as follows:
1. Estimate the total income and the proportion available for departmental expenditure (63 per cent).
2. Use the allocation of funded home load between cost centres from the Plan.
3. Calculate the national average units of departmental expenditure for each cost centre and each unit in the formula, and increase to allow for inflation.
4. Use a UFC type formula with the following components:
   (a) 60 per cent for teaching on weighted student load: ug : pgt : pgr = 1 : 1.5 : 2
   (b) 15 per cent for research judgement: average = 1; below average = 0.25; above average = 1.5; outstanding = 2.
   (c) An overhead of 26 per cent on expenditure from Research Councils and Charities.
   (d) The balance for research on weighted student load; ug : pgt : pgr = 1 : 2 : 4.
   (e) An overhead of 4.55 per cent on other research grants and contracts.
       (ug = undergraduate; pgt = postgraduate student; pgr = postgraduate research student)
5. Add in the following income from overseas and associate students:
   (a) 60 per cent of fee income from overseas and associate undergraduate load.
   (b) 70 per cent of fee income from overseas taught postgraduate load.
   (c) 85 per cent of fee income from overseas research postgraduate load.
6. Deduct loss of fee income for any shortfall in funded student load and add in any additional fee income for any excess home postgraduates.
7. Scale the total to equal the resource available.

Table 3.2   Procedures for departmental allocations: in university B

Departments make bids for resources based on their own estimates a year at a time. Allocations are made on a judgemental basis as 'the Vice-Chancellor is not keen on formula funding'. Departmental grants are tightly controlled and there is a move to make the departments responsible for more areas of expenditure – light and heat, postage, telephone – in addition to normal consumable expenditure. The University is thinking of charging them for space but nothing has been done yet. Pay costs are controlled centrally – and very tightly – by the Vice-Chancellor, apart from some short term posts.

There are no restrictions on departments raising money and indeed departments are encouraged to be entrepreneurial by the use of incentives as additions to their basic grants, e.g.:

(a) 2.5 per cent of overseas student fees.
(b) 35 per cent of overseas fees above a threshold fixed in 1980/81 (when the new overseas policy came into force). This is gradually being phased out by the reduction of the threshold in consideration of departments bearing the cost of staff on their departmental votes.
(c) 7.5 per cent of the previous year's income from grants from Research Councils and Charities (i.e. those that do not pay overheads).
(d) 20 per cent of fee income from occasional students (on less than one year's course).
(e) An incentive for recruitment to the preparatory course for overseas students.
(f) 50 per cent of the overheads from contract research.

Surpluses on 'centre activities' are usually divided 50 : 50 with the University centrally. Some of a centre's share may be split with its associated departments.

Table 3.3   Departmental formula for departmental allocations: in university C

The formula vote allocation for any department, centre or unit is as follows:

$$FV = a + by + cy + dy + ey + fy + g + h + i + jy = + k$$

Where:

FV = Formula vote

a = basic allowance = 0 for departments, centres of biotechnology and environmental technology, £K20 for all other centres and units.

b = UG (3-year) = DW × UG (3-year) load.

c = UG (4-year) = 1.15 × DW × UG (4-year) load.

d = PG advanced course, academic-year = DW × PG(C) Academic-year load.

e = PG advanced course, calendar-year = 1.35 × DW × PG(C) calendar-year load.

f = PG research = 2.00 × DW × PG(R) load.

g = Overseas fees element = 15 per cent of each overseas student's fee.

h = Research grant element = 40 per cent of gross expenditure based on a three-year average × 0.75.

i = Research contract element = departmental share of 8.5 per cent of the College's gross expenditure on a previous-year basis × 0.75.

j = Field work element = DW × field work FTE student load × 1.15.

k = Research selectivity element = an allocation from £K500 based on the research-related elements of the vote formula (current-year basis) weighted by a scale related to the UGC's assessment of research in May 1986 × 0.75.

y = Capitation grant.

DW = Departmental weighting = 1 except for mathematics, the school of management, and environmental technology where it is 0.7.

UG = Undergraduate; PG = Post-graduate.

services, 60 per cent of the remaining UFC grant is allocated for teaching and 40 per cent for research performance. Allocations for teaching are based on student numbers weighted by level of study. The research element is based essentially on an allocation of most of the overhead component of Research Council grants, a share of research contract income and a selectivity element based upon the UGC assessment of the strength of the department.

In another university also with full devolution to departments the funding formula allocated 64 per cent of the UFC block grant and overseas student fee income to departmental cost centres and 36 per cent was top-sliced for central administration and services. Of the money allocated to departments 60 per cent went to teaching, 25 per cent unselectively for research and 15 per cent selectively for research which includes a component of 'research potential which may not yet be reflected in realised research income and output'. In another university with full devolution the allocation per student in departmental allocations is not necessarily the same as that used by the UFC. However the university 'does take seriously the science and technology/non-science division of resources and students, although even here the relative student weights are not necessarily those used by the UFC'.

Another formula is largely student number based, weightings being given for taught and research postgraduates. The formula contains a 'budget centre factor' which is a judgemental component to take account of the special needs of particular departments and 'this may vary between departments by a factor of 10 determined largely on the basis of historical precedents'. In addition to the formula allocation, departments are given incentives for such income earning activities as the recruitment of overseas students, a share of overheads on research contracts or a share of the DR portion of the UFC grant, i.e. that part reckoned to be attributable to income from the Research Councils and charities. In total, departments receive between 25 per cent and 30 per cent of the income presumed to be attributable to the DR allocation. This is an example of a university with a substantial deficit and savings targets are agreed for each cost centre and the appropriate share of overheads or incentive allowances is withheld from a cost centre if its savings target is not met. The budgets for staff are given in the form of established posts rather than monetary allocations and 'in order to meet the contractual obligations to permanent staff the sources available to departments are top-sliced by the amount of academic salaries before the remainder is allocated to cost centres'.

In a university with little financial devolution departmental grants are calculated on the basis of FTE students weighted by subject area. The system was described as being based on the UGC model but 'only as a guide not as a rigid system'. Science and Humanities weightings are standard but in other areas they have been decided *ad hoc*. When the results of the UGC/UFC research selectivity exercise became known, the university 're-tuned its allocation of research money to reflect each department's performance'. In this university departments retain 50 per cent of any overheads they earn from research contracts. The university has considered introducing a greater degree of devolution of financial responsibility to cost centres but has so far decided against any significant move in this direction. Staffing is tightly controlled from the centre by a Resources Committee, and differential student–staff ratios are calculated in terms of the JR (judgemental research) element in the recurrent grant.

In another university with relatively low central administrative costs which has retained centralized financial regulation and control the Vice-Chancellor believed that 'if the university went for devolved financial responsibilities to faculties there would be a considerable increase in expense. The Registrar considered that departments are headed by 'an independent-minded bunch who already feel loaded with bureaucracy, and the world ought to be a simpler place'.

PCFC institutions

In the non-university sector most of the information obtained during the survey concerned intentions following incorporation. Of the ten institutions all but one small college intended to implement some financial devolution to faculties, schools or departments. However, the proposed extent varied considerably. Three of the eight polytechnics hoped to undertake substantial financial devolution to schools or faculties but not departments. In one polytechnic which leases a considerable amount of space the administration intended in addition to charge cost centres for the use of teaching rooms. In the other six non-university institutions some devolution of non-staff budgets was planned during the first 12 months of corporate status. One reason often given for not devolving financial responsibility for academic staff was doubts about the capacity of devolved cost centres to make the necessary cuts at a time when the institutions were expected to face substantial deficits. This contrasts with the claim reported above that in some universities devolution of financial responsibilities is in practice a devolution of responsibility for implementing budget cuts.

It was pointed out by one of the polytechnic respondents that if departments receive funding on a historical basis, financial devolution in a period of financial stringency leads to random cuts. This was the case, one respondent claimed, in several public sector institutions in the early 1980s. All the polytechnics which were moving in the direction of financial devolution were proposing to use formula based systems of allocation. It was expected that the influence of strategic planning would appear at the stage where the initial allocations are made to departments. Activities which the institutional managers wish to give preferential treatment, were to receive higher weightings in the formulae. An example of procedures being adopted in polytechnics is given in Table 3.4.

Devolution and virement

In all the case study institutions laboratories, workshops and offices were allocated to departments centrally, usually on a long-term basis, though in one university 'all space is, in principle, reallocated annually'. While there has been a move towards central booking of lecture and seminar rooms in order to use space more efficiently only in one of the polytechnics was there a 'possibility of charging departments for the use of space' for general teaching and research purposes, though all include a charge for space in the costing of income generating activities. It was widely accepted that rooms are often idle at less popular periods but so far no scheme has been devised for differential charges for peak and off peak use.

The biggest problem for schemes of financial devolution is academic staff salaries. They account for 72 per cent of departmental expenditure in universities: in Humanities and Law the figure is 90 per cent. Thus if responsibility for academic salaries is devolved and funds are allocated to departments on the basis of formulae such as those previously discussed, an average sized Humanities cost centre (20 staff) that replaced a retiring lecturer with a new lecturer at the bottom of the scale would find itself with a windfall profit equivalent to a 30 per cent increase in its disposable cash. In a fully devolved financial system the age and experience of a

Table 3.4   Proposed resource allocation procedures: polytechnic A

The main contracts will be between the teaching departments, the faculties and the central departments. All income derived from the teaching process will be allocated to departments, e.g. PCFC income, overseas student income, short-course income, tuition fees, etc. on the basis of enrolled and taught student numbers. A proportion of that income will then be allocated to the faculty in respect of services it provides to the departments within it, and to the central departments in respect of services provided to the departments/faculties by contract.

For teaching departments income will be determined as follows:

(a) In respect of PCFC income on the basis of the agreed academic plan as submitted to the funding body, calculated on the basis of the previous year's unit of resource adjusted for an estimate of inflation.

(b) Non-advanced further education on the basis of local authority agreements negotiated annually.

(c) Tuition fee income on the basis of the academic plan and the previous year's fee levels adjusted for an estimate of inflation.

(d) Overseas student fee income on the basis of previous year's numbers and fees adjusted for estimated inflation.

(e) Short course income on the basis of departmental targets.

In each case actual income levels will be used, if known, and estimates would be adjusted when actuals are determined. Total Polytechnic income would also be calculated having regard to purely centrally derived income (e.g. rents, interest earned, library fines, etc.).

---

department's academic staff, which are matters largely outside its control, have a powerful gearing effect on the resources available for other activities.

Nevertheless four universities *had* devolved responsibilities for academic staff salaries to departments or faculties. In three of these the devolved budgets amounted in practice to staff saving targets, with most of any income saved from staff resignations contributing to the reduction of departmental deficits. Devolution was in effect a way of bringing certain performance indicators to the notice of academic staff at departmental level.

Similar considerations apply to the salaries of support staff although obviously to a lesser extent. The average percentage of expenditure on support staff salaries for all cost centres in 1987/88 was 19 per cent in universities and 16 per cent in polytechnics. However, a more relevant indicator in many ways is they account for about two thirds of all departmental expenditure other than academic salaries. Thus once academic staff salaries have been met, support staff salaries are almost as large a part of the remaining expenditure as academic salaries are of total expenditure. Thus in institutions with no devolution of academic salaries the arguments against the devolution of support staff salaries are almost equally strong.

This suggests that devolution should either include all salaries or no salaries and this is what we observed in most cases. All institutions with devolved responsibility for academic staff give devolved cost centres the financial responsibility for support staff as well. In three others departmental budgets included an allowance for non-academic salaries. In most, however, departments have an 'establishment' of technicians, secretaries and other support staff; and permission to fill vacancies has to be sought centrally. In all cases, the university, polytechnic or college, as the employing body, was responsible for the terms and conditions of service.

In all but three of the universities departments were responsible for postage and telephone charges. One of the others had a pilot monitoring scheme in operation so that charges to departments could be introduced when appropriate. In the non-university institutions there was little explicit charging for postage and telephones, but this was to be part of the devolution in those which were planning it.

One test of the extent of financial devolution is the extent to which cost centres are able to move funds between budget heads. The case study institutions covered the whole spectrum, from one in which cost centres had virtually complete freedom to another in which specific approval had to be obtained for all but the smallest purchases outside those budgeted for.

As has been shown, devolution of responsibility for academic salaries with the possibility of virement between academic salaries and other expenditures can result in very large, almost random, differences between departments in their disposable funds. It was suggested in one university, that a department might be reluctant to put staff forward for promotion if it was already short of funds, and that this would lead to inequities and loss of collegiality.

Compared with salaries, virement between other budget heads poses few problems and was permitted in all but two of the case study institutions where departments and faculties have little significant budgetary responsibility.

Carrying over surpluses and deficits is virement over time. It is permitted in all the institutions with devolved budgets but in most universities it appeared only in the 1980s and it was not possible in public sector institutions when they were governed by local authority financial regulations. The disadvantage is that it represents further loss of direct control by the centre. A department with an accumulated surplus can carry on spending money even if the rest of the institution is in deficit. The advantage is that departments are not encouraged to spend their whole allocation before some arbitrary budgetary deadline, while those with deficits do not in effect have them remitted each year. However, there are problems. In most places it is not thought desirable to allow unlimited accumulation of either surpluses or deficits. The usual procedure is to allow surpluses up to some predetermined limit, while deficits that are large or chronic result in intervention from the centre.

Nine of the fourteen universities visited were expecting to incur substantial deficits during the early 1990s. In this situation departmental surpluses and deficits amount to little more than a key performance indicator showing which activities ought to be discontinued. We were told explicitly in one university that the only effective performance indicator for departments now when making claims for staff or facilities is this 'bottom line'.

Number of cost centres

While it is apparent from the above discussion that most higher education institutions are moving rapidly in the direction of financial devolution there are considerable differences of opinion about the appropriate size and number of the cost centres. Discussions hinge on three considerations:

1. The number of units the central administration can conveniently deal with.
2. The optimum size of cost centres taking into account management information needs and the capacity of departmental managers to interpret it.
3. The extent of financial devolution.

In establishing schemes of financial devolution most attention has been paid to the number of budget holders within the institution. Several senior administrators and institutional heads referred to span of management control, that is the number of people who can reasonably be given direct access to central management. There seems to be a widespread belief that 10–20 is the appropriate number whatever the size of institution. In one large university a new Vice-Chancellor whose previous career had been outside universities remarked that the 120 departments in the university was far too many to coordinate effectively on a devolved basis while the existing nine faculties was too few. He was hoping to establish about 16 budget centres based on groupings of departments. Amongst the universities with significant financial devolution one has between 25 and 30 semi-autonomous cost centres. No other has more than 16. The smallest number, in a very large university, is 12.

Consideration of the appropriate size of departmental cost centre invariably takes second place to the issue of the number of them. There has been some discussion of the issue but the size of cost centres varies considerably within and between institutions. Minimum size seems to be determined by senior management's perceptions of the availability of management skills amongst middle managers. In one institution with little devolution it was conceded by senior managers that there were two 'mega departments with several dozen staff each and considerable external income, which could well operate as independent cost centres within a budget determined centrally'.

In only a few institutions are administrative support staff a consideration, although there is some acknowledgement that if departmental or faculty cost centres are to have major management responsibilities, it is necessary for them to have access to specialist administrators. Even less explicit attention has been given to maximum size of cost centre than to minimum size. There was some recognition that if the management unit is too large, many of the anticipated benefits of devolution are lost. Some academics retain the idea of a department as a group of individuals in closely related subject and disciplinary areas who can conveniently meet in a single room to discuss, rather than to debate, at least the broad issues of departmental priorities and management. However, in many cases, particularly in scientific and technological areas, this is obviously no longer possible and departments themselves have management structures within them.

Conclusions

This study is not concerned with institutional administration in itself but only in so far as it is influenced by external funding. From this viewpoint, it is apparent that a variety of internal management structures have proved to be viable in coping with turbulent financial circumstances. The essential consideration is for institutions to have mechanisms for establishing realistic priorities, implementing strategic plans and ensuring that resources are not used inefficiently or wastefully. It is also important for there to be systems of incentives, both carrots and sticks, to encourage individuals and small groups to undertake activities for the benefit of the institution as a whole. In the present financial and political climate this includes the generation of income from a wide variety of sources to help maintain financial viability. It is generally believed that financial devolution helps to achieve this by making the relationship between effort and reward as direct as possible. However, a few universities have shown that financial as well as academic success can be achieved with a high degree of centralized management and financial regulation, provided that institutional loyalties are well developed and there are excellent two way flows of management information.

4

External Income Generation

Introduction

Earned income can be a source of both profit and problems. Successful management of soft money means encouraging the establishment of systems and procedures that help to realize the profit and avoid the problems.

Since 1980, an increasing proportion of the income of higher education institutions has been directly 'earned' through the sale of specific academic and other services. If student fees are included as part of this earned income, it now amounts to well over half of the income of some universities and in 1989/90 about 47 per cent of the recurrent income of the university sector as a whole. In 1992 following the government decision to transfer substantial funds away from the UFC to student fee subsidy and to research councils the percentage of income that is 'earned' in this sense is likely to rise to nearly 70 per cent. The percentage in the non-university sector is lower at about 25 per cent and this is likely to rise to at least 40 per cent. In part this much lower figure in PCFC institutions resulted from the control of institutional finance by local authorities until 1989. The reported percentage of external income can confidently be expected to increase considerably following incorporation, partly because the polytechnics and colleges have greater encouragement to generate income now that they can retain it for their own use, and partly because institutional managers are now keen to bring as much reported income as possible within the central institutional accounts.

Categories of income

There are, broadly, six ways in which academic institutions can supplement their core income: gifts, investments, research grants, research contracts, consultancy and student fees. Donations and investment income are part of general institutional income and usually tend to reinforce centralist management structures, but all the others are related to specific activities within institutions and tend to strengthen those departments and groups which are able to earn them.

Gifts

In 1988/89 income from gifts, endowments and donations averaged 1.5 per cent of total recurrent income of British universities, ranging from 5.5 per cent in Oxford University to 0.5 per cent or less in 14 universities. The nature of public sector financing till 1989/90 made it much more difficult to obtain similar figures from polytechnics and colleges but amongst the case study institutions from which we were able to obtain figures it was never more than 0.1 per cent of recurrent income. Several universities (but, amongst the case study institutions, no polytechnics or colleges) were launching appeals for funds to support general academic activities.

Investment income

Portfolio management is a significant responsibility of finance officers in most institutions. Amongst the case study universities an average of just over 2 per cent of total recurrent income in 1988 came from interest on investments and short-term deposits. Most universities were clustered around this 2 per cent figure but there were a few extreme cases on either side ranging from 0.1 per cent to 3.4 per cent. In all but two of the universities investment income was greater than that from continuing education and full cost courses. Again the non-university figure was typically much lower. However, in one of our case-study polytechnics investment income in 1988 was 2.5 per cent of total recurrent income and in another 1.8 per cent. Both were inner London polytechnics which already had responsibility for their own financial affairs. Conversely, in a polytechnic in the north of England the figure was 0.05 per cent.

Research

In 1988/89 just over 20 per cent of the total recurrent income of UK universities consisted of research grants and contracts: it had risen from less than 13 per cent in 1980/81. Within departmental cost centres the proportion of total recurrent expenditure that comes from research grants and contracts varies from more than 52 per cent in clinical medicine to 3 per cent in law. Of the total income from research 34 per cent was from research councils in 1988/89 compared with 46 per cent in 1981/82. The proportion of polytechnic income from research in 1987/88 was 5.9 per cent, of which 10 per cent was from research councils.

The biggest single difference between universities and polytechnics in their responses to questions about financial management concerns the role of the dual support system whereby a significant part of the UFC grant reinforces research council funding. Dual funding has enabled universities to compete for research council grants on more favourable terms than polytechnics and colleges which, not surprisingly, universally perceive it as being unfair. The universities, on the other hand, almost equally universally, claim that further erosion of the principle of dual funding will cause irreparable damage to research and scholarship, though some research-oriented university staff believe research would benefit if all research income were allocated by the research councils. The future of dual funding will be one of the most difficult issues to resolve when the PCFC and the UFC are merged.

As a result of dual funding, grants to universities from research councils and charities have been funded on a direct costs-only basis. The research council meets only the payroll costs of research staff and other direct project costs.[1] It is assumed that the university already has a 'well-found' laboratory, office and computer facilities, administrative back-up and academic staff who will supervise the research. The UFC's DR contribution helps to cover these items but the UFC does not indicate how it is to be split between the different 'overhead' activities, and there are widespread claims that it does not recompense universities for the full costs of Research Council grants. There are wide differences between universities in the way this 'Direct Research (DR) element' of the UFC grant has been shared between central services and departmental cost centres. In several there are sharply different perceptions between academic departments and university central administrations about what does happen. It is a frequent source of complaint by departmental and research centre managers.

Several universities levy an overhead charge of between 15 per cent and 35 per cent of any externally funded research project and the remainder is available for the cost centre where the research is done. In the case of research council grants this means that the university adds to the budget of the departmental cost centre an amount equivalent to between 5 per cent and 15 per cent of the value of the research council grant. Some such procedure is frequently built into formulae determining departmental allocations as one of the weights.

Obviously universities with a large amount of financial devolution to departmental cost centres allocate larger sums to departments in respect of DR on Research Council grants than those where financial decisions are centralized. One university's formula effectively returns to departments an amount equivalent to 30 per cent of research council grant whereas in a university with virtually no financial devolution, nothing is returned automatically but research performance has a significant influence on the annual departmental allocations.

The picture is very different in the PCFC institutions. Several polytechnic directors and finance officers commented that research council grants were a mixed blessing. While they are pleased to receive them because of the prestige they confer, they are seen to be using institutional resources which ought to be available for teaching. One Director expressed doubts, not entirely tongue-in-cheek, about the legality of accepting Research Council grants in that it implies the commitment of funds that should be used for teaching. However, apart from a very few projects in engineering and technology, most of the Research Council work in the polytechnics is on a small scale compared with the universities. It is universally claimed in polytechnics that this is a direct result of the absence of dual support in their core funding.

Costing research contracts

The essential difference between a research grant and a research contract is that the former is initiated by the researcher to pursue some academic objective and is to some extent subsidized out of general institutional funds, while the latter is usually initiated by the sponsor and is expected to cover its full costs. In practice, research contracts cover most of the research and development work undertaken for organizations other than research councils and charitable trusts and foundations together with a small amount of research council work. Between 1981/82 and 1988/89 research income other than from research councils grew from 6.8 per cent to 13.0 per cent of total university income.

Research contract income has been the subject of considerable attention in both universities and polytechnics. The issues surrounding it encapsulate the debate about higher education funding that is likely to be generalized as the UFC and PCFC establish funding arrangements that are broadly contractual in nature and research councils contribute a larger proportion of the full costs of research they sponsor.

Until the early 1980s, the distinction in universities between research grants and contracts was blurred and was not separately reported in the published statistics. While there was undoubtedly a distinction in the minds of most university staff between research that arose out of their academic interests, and research initiated and commissioned by clients in order to find solutions to particular problems of interest to the client, the notion of profitability hardly existed and was generally considered to be rather unethical to try to push costs too high.

Since the mid-1980s the issue of full cost pricing of research and consultancy has received considerable attention, and this concern will undoubtedly increase. Much of the debate appears to be about technical accounting matters but accounting conventions are often rigorous and precise statements of broader and more fundamental concepts. The technical issues are concerned essentially with the question, '*How* does a university or polytechnic determine the real cost of undertaking a particular piece of paid work?' The more fundamental issues are concerned with the question, '*Why should* an academic institution undertake a particular piece of paid work?'.

If all the activities of a university or polytechnic are funded on a contractual basis all need to make an appropriate contribution to the institution's overheads if it is to be economically viable in the long run. The CVCP guide to the costing of research contracts, *The Costing of Research and Projects in Universities* (1988), is widely quoted. The guidelines on pricing distinguish between *costing* and *pricing*. Prices must be determined by what the market will bear. The purpose of detailed costing is to determine whether what the market will bear is economically worthwhile. The central recommendation of the CVCP Guidelines is that academic staff salaries account for about 45 per cent of the total expenditure of British Universities and that, therefore, the payroll should be multiplied by about 2.2 in order for any project to make its proper contribution to institutional costs. All universities have taken steps to attempt to implement them at least to the extent of trying to make academics bidding for research contracts aware of the true costs.

The European Community has also regulations for the payment of indirect costs concerned with its projects under the COMETT Programme. Under the EC procedures all universities must opt for one of two schemes for the payment of indirect costs. They may either claim a composite overhead amounting to 50 per cent of direct costs or they must include as many indirect costs as possible, in which case they are allowed a 20 per cent 'overhead'. While one or two universities, with experience of the EC, were, at the time of the interviews, having little difficulty with these guidelines they were causing considerable confusion in most as they were obviously not consistent with the CVCP recommendations. This is not surprising. The CVCP can be considered to be a cartel of providers of research while the EC is a major purchaser.

A critical difference between the CVCP guidelines and those of the European Community, and the critical accounting issue in the costing of externally funded projects is to determine which of the activities of the university or polytechnic it is legitimate to include as part of the indirect costs of any activity. The CVCP guidelines implicitly assume that the whole of the central administration and services of a university are necessary for all the activities it undertakes, while the EC is concerned to identify the costs of overhead activities which are essential for a university or polytechnic to function as a research institution. Organizations in which the principal function is contract research have different administrative structures and central service provision from those where the prime function is the teaching of undergraduate students. The university registry, for example, is primarily concerned with student affairs. Many other services – such as libraries and learning resources centres, educational media services, sports facilities and lecture room space – are also required primarily for undergraduate teaching and are not part of the infrastructure needed for research. Several of the institutions visited were undertaking, or were about to undertake, or felt they needed to undertake, a comprehensive costing exercise to assess the real cost of their various activities, but none was able to show the results of such a study.

Despite all these attempts at finding a basis for full-cost pricing the commonest practice in both universities and polytechnics is the UFC assumption that, for most average sized research council projects, a reasonable approximation to full recurrent cost would be obtained by adding about 40 per cent to the direct costs. This was originally based on a regression analysis which showed that universities' total costs increased by 40 per cent of the additional departmental costs of research projects. In many institutions, both universities and polytechnics, this figure has become a target for all research projects.

Pricing policies are, however, complicated by the fact that for academics the prime objective is usually not immediate financial profit. They take on contract work because it enables them to do research and other work activities that they want to do anyway; or because it serves the function of promotional advertising, or of establishing contacts with firms or other enterprises that may produce students or larger research contracts in the future or simply because some of it is thought to feed through to influence UFC research ratings. Sometimes contract work may be seen as career development, providing opportunities for staff, and students, to broaden their experience of work outside academia.

It is possible to construct a league table of implicit overhead recovery on research projects by comparing research income with direct research expenditure in each university cost centre. Income from research councils and charities must be excluded because the indirect costs associated with these projects were included in the UGC grant. Table 4.1 shows that in the mid 1980s less than 9 per cent of the income universities received from research contracts was available to meet indirect and overhead costs. Finance offices in all the universities visited were aware of such league tables and were taking steps to improve their ranking within them. In 1989 the percentage had risen to nearly 13 per cent but it was widely agreed that did not nearly meet the full costs of housing most research projects. The case study institutions included some near the top and some near the bottom of the list. The institutions near the top of the list were much more likely than those at the bottom to have made concerted efforts to ensure that negotiations for research contracts adhered rigorously to costing guidelines.

The costing and pricing of contract work is creating tensions, sometimes severe, between departments and central administration. The view of departmental staff is that they undertake research work primarily because it is academically worthwhile, or because it generates income that enables them to undertake other activities that are academically worthwhile. The central administration, and particularly the finance office, is more concerned with the question of how the full costs of the research or teaching are to be met. When substantial indirect costs are recovered academics in

Table 4.1   Estimated overhead recovery rates (%)

	1984/85	1988/89
Salford	33.99	40.27
London Business School	16.09	26.19
Loughborough	14.92	23.35
Aston	9.76	21.66
Sheffield	16.89	19.90
East Anglia	0.00	19.47
Birmingham	7.67	18.89
Durham	13.50	18.78
Warwick	12.93	17.72
Southampton	13.48	17.14
Bath	14.35	17.13
Reading	7.52	16.81
Oxford	14.77	16.77
Nottingham	−0.15	16.76
Bristol	13.65	16.57
Lancaster	0.00	16.20
York	12.04	16.11
Bradford	10.06	15.26
Brunel	8.73	15.25
Kent	0.00	14.41
Swansea	14.68	14.18
City	18.03	14.13
Sussex	5.07	13.63
Leeds	10.49	13.55
Surrey	0.00	13.27
Cardiff	0.00	13.16
Stirling	2.91	13.09
Keele	0.00	12.74
Hull	14.71	12.32
Newcastle	12.11	12.10
Dundee	0.00	11.79
Liverpool	5.77	11.79
London	7.47	11.70
Leicester	9.49	11.48
Essex	6.61	11.28
Cambridge	12.33	10.98
Heriot-Watt	0.70	10.91
Exeter	10.82	10.87
Aberdeen	5.71	10.34
Manchester	8.98	10.23
Bangor	9.35	10.04
Belfast	0.00	8.54
St Andrews	6.35	8.39
Edinburgh	7.94	8.34
UMIST	12.33	8.20
Strathclyde	5.47	6.94
Ulster	0.00	6.09
University of Wales College of Medicine	3.38	3.17
Aberystwyth	0.00	3.09
Lampeter	0.00	2.20
Glasgow	3.96	2.12
UK Total	8.78	12.83

Source: *University Statistics 1984/85 and 1988/89 Vol. 3: Finance.*

the departments who have earned them often resent these surpluses going to what they see as unnecessary central administration or to subsidize less active departments. This tension appeared in some form in all the case study institutions.

The much more fundamental issue is the rationale for income generating activities at all. One view is that a university, polytechnic or college exists to teach undergraduate and postgraduate students and to pursue scholarship and basic research, and that these should be paid for collectively out of public funds because the market is unable to provide teaching and research equitably and efficiently. Anything else detracts from these real functions and is justified only if it generates a surplus which can be used to advance teaching and research. To some extent this is the premise on which Table 4.1 is based. The income of a higher education institution consists of those general funds which are available for teaching or research at its own discretion plus any grants from research councils or charitable trusts. Any other activities are undertaken in order to provide a surplus that can be made available for general academic use. This is still the majority view amongst the university finance officers we interviewed and it is probably the view of the majority of university and polytechnic academic staff, though many of the staff who are active in applied research, consultancy and full cost course provision believe they have academic value over and above any 'profit' they generate.

The alternative view is that universities and polytechnics are economic enterprises in the knowledge industry, and it is appropriate for them to sell whatever mix of academic services is most cost-effective. Before 1980 there was no doubt that conventional undergraduate and postgraduate courses, paid for out of public funds, were the most profitable activities and, therefore, issues about whether or not it was proper to pursue other business were of marginal significance. Even when universities used some resources to provide public services – such as the time of academic staff spent on government committees, or adult education programmes, or providing concerts for the local community – these were deemed to be both marginal and supportive of real academic work.

If core public funding of teaching and research is insufficient to maintain its existing size and organizational structure an institution has the choice of contracting until it is viable within its core resources, or of expanding its income from other sources. This is obvious enough. However, dilemmas occur when staff are employed specifically for income generation as, for example, as employees of academic companies. It implies either a recognition that such work is now part of the mainstream business of the university or polytechnic, or else that the staff paid to do it are essentially hired labourers whose function is to generate a surplus so that established teaching and research staff can have the time to carry out the real academic work of the institution.

If contract work is treated as being equivalent to the more traditional academic work this implies a recognition that the university as it has developed over the past century at least has irrevocably changed. Few polytechnics and hardly any universities are yet prepared to embrace this change wholeheartedly. It certainly raises some delicate questions. At what point does a university or polytechnic providing consultancy and similar services become a consultancy firm that also provides some degree courses? At what stage does competition from institutions with charitable status become unfair to other enterprises operating in similar areas?

Consultancy

Organized institutional consultancy was one of the innovations of the 1980s. Ten of the 14 case study universities and all of the polytechnics had some form of institutional consultancy service that aimed to function as a profit making enterprise. In a few there was concern that institutional consultancies were being undercut by the longer established practice of private staff consultancies. We were told of cases in which government departments had encouraged conflicts of loyalty by seeking to persuade individual academics to undertake personal rather than institutional consultancy in order to avoid overhead charges. In most institutions with devolved budgetary responsibility it is widely expected that members of academic staff will contribute at least part of their individual consultancy earnings to help overcome departmental deficits.

Consultancy is one stage further than contract research from `core academic activities. Even here, however, the boundary is not clear cut. Consultancy is normally undertaken primarily for financial gain, but it is also justified in terms of opportunities for practical professional experience for academic staff or students, and as a promotional activity to attract subsequent research contracts.

Consultancy is usually costed on the basis of staff time and there is a wide variety of practices. Average daily consultancy rates charged by universities and polytechnics ranged from about £150 to about £500 in 1989. However, it was accepted that there were individual cases where both more and less than this amount was charged, if the market would bear it. Some Social Studies and Education Departments claimed that there were problems in selling consultancy services to public authorities, especially local authorities, even at the lower end of this price range though, in practice, Education Departments are particularly active in this kind of work (see for example Loder, 1992).

Private consultancy by academic staff has been a matter of debate for many years. Its existence is widely acknowledged but there is virtually no reliable information of its extent or distribution. A study in the early 1970s (Williams *et al.*, 1974) showed that on average university teachers admitted to increasing their basic salary by about 12.5 per cent from supplementary earnings of various kinds. But it was spread very unevenly: more than half the respondents claimed to have no external earnings at all, implying that the remainder were able to increase their income by 25 per cent on average. There have been no more recent published studies of private consultancy earnings although they are referred to from time to time in connection with salary negotiations.

A distinction is often made between long established academic perquisites and newer forms of consultancy. The former includes book royalties, external examining fees and payments for public lectures. These are generally held to be wholly compatible with academic duties and in most cases individuals retain any income earned after reimbursement of costs incurred by the institution. Occasionally, there is an informal agreement to share it with the department or other individuals within it. Television and radio appearances seem for the most part to have been added to this list of 'legitimate' academic activities. Other kinds of private consultancy involving contracts of some kind with industry or government cause greater concern. Well over half the institutions we visited had recently established guidelines or revised them, or were in the process of doing so, to draw clear boundaries between legitimate private enterprise and institutional commitments.

A view that is gaining ascendancy in PCFC institutions and a few universities is that individual academics have contractual commitments to their universities or polytechnics for a certain number of hours per year. New contracts of employment often require members of staff to be available for work in their institutions for specified periods and any income earned during these periods belongs to the institution, though incentive payments are often made to individuals who generate supplementary income.

The more traditional view is that individuals have a responsibility to make adequate contributions to teaching, research and administration, and provided they meet these commitments satisfactorily they are free to undertake outside paid work using their professional knowledge and skills. This tends to be the dominant view in universities but it is somewhat blurred in practice because only very rarely are there specified norms for the amount of teaching and research that are expected from individuals. In most universities private consultancy is a matter, that in principle, has to be authorized by the Vice-Chancellor: senior administrators are confident that any consultancy requiring substantial absence from the university will be known by the head of department and the head of institution. In several universities a day a week was considered an acceptable maximum. This rule of thumb also seems to have some sanction in other European countries (Barnes, 1989). However, it is equally apparent that there is a substantial amount of smaller scale consultancy which is not reported and which universities and polytechnics have hitherto made little attempt to monitor.

The general view in most universities is that, with few exceptions, the amount of income made available to the institution from any formal 'taxing' of small-scale private consultancy would be less than the costs resulting from loss of staff morale if extra effort by individuals is seen to be penalized.

The justification for what was described by one respondent as 'this relaxed approach' is fourfold:

1. The total amount of such private consultancy is marginal and the aggravation caused by attempting to monitor it centrally would outweigh any benefits from diverting some of the income into general institutional funds.
2. Normal collegial checks and balance within a department will prevent a situation arising whereby some individuals obtain substantial outside earnings and in so doing impose significant extra work on their colleagues.
3. In some disciplines – engineering and business studies/computing were frequently mentioned in this respect – consultancy is one of the ways in which teachers and researchers keep in contact with the professional activities they are teaching and studying. It is, in effect, a form of free staff development; and if it did not exist it would be necessary to invent it. Indeed, it might be said that in some cases, it *has* been found necessary to invent it through various programmes of industrial contacts such as the Enterprise in Higher Education Initiative.
4. Consultancy opportunities are most frequent in those areas where it is most difficult to recruit staff. Authorization of private consultancy is one of the ways in which labour market pressures can be accommodated without abandoning general salary scales that cover all academic staff. Williams *et al.* (1974) drew attention to the way in which external earnings helped bring about an equilibrium between demand and supply of highly qualified academic staff, within a framework of standardized national salary scales applied to individuals with a wide variety of specialist skills, who face very different labour market demands for their services.

One matter that causes some concern is legal liability for private consultancy work. Some institutions require individuals to sign a formal disclaimer of any institutional liability for private work they undertake.

In concluding this section on paid external work a related matter of concern to many academics is worth mentioning: the pressures on the unpaid external work they have traditionally done, such as refereeing for research funding bodies and for academic journals, serving on committees for public authorities and honorary work for learned societies and professional bodies. There is a widespread feeling that unless such activities are explicitly recognized in individual and institutional performance indicators they will inevitably receive low priority and the quality of work and hence the general intellectual environment will decline.

Fees

There are three broad sources of fees: home students on regular courses, overseas students and full-cost courses.

Fees from home students on regular undergraduate and postgraduate courses did not figure prominently in institutional financial strategies during the 1980s. The relatively high fees of the late 1970s resulted in additional fees-only students being recruited by some universities and polytechnics because fees were higher than short-run marginal costs. This was not the case from 1981 onwards and; with a few exceptions, home student fees were treated simply as an alternative channel for supplementary funds from central government, over which the institution had little control.

The increases in fees in the 1990s are intended to change these attitudes and will undoubtedly do so. Many institutions are finding it worthwhile to recruit fees-only students even though the long-run effect of this will undoubtedly be to lower average expenditure per student. In two of the case study universities 'premium fees' were being charged to students on some business studies courses. Apart from these examples, we received no evidence that charging what the market will bear was being seriously considered.

However, by 1989 higher educational institutions had nearly a decade to familiarize themselves with the implication of full-cost fees for overseas students. Chapter 6 shows how most universities rapidly adopted active marketing strategies in the early 1980s and by the end of the decade most polytechnics were doing the same. Income from overseas student fees comprises nearly 6 per cent of the recurrent income of British Universities and in four it accounts for more than 10 per cent. In several universities in 1989 this was seen as the largest single component of income over which the institution had some control. It is not, therefore, surprising that overseas student recruitment was described as their most professionally organized marketing activity by administrators in several universities.

Full-cost short course fees are of rapidly growing importance in most institutions and in 1988/89 accounted for 2.2 per cent of the income of universities. They bear a similar relationship to teaching as consultancies do to research and they present similar practical and theoretical problems. Are they appropriate in higher education institutions? What is their relationship to mainstream activities? How can income from short courses be allocated in an efficient and equitable way? Chapter 7 is concerned with Continuing Education and these issues are discussed there.

Note

1 This was changed in September 1991 and research councils are now able to pay an indirect cost of up to 40 per cent.

5

Organization and Management of Income Generation

Introduction

Academic institutions manage their income generating enterprises in three main ways:

1. Encouraging academic departments to undertake consultancy and full cost course provision as part of their regular portfolio of activities.
2. Setting up research and development centres or units that are administered by the institution.
3. Establishing limited companies that have a legal status separate from the parent institution.

Even in institutions with little devolution of financial responsibility for general funds, academic departments often have a discretionary financial account for their income generating activities. In many respects, this is an extension of the long-established practice whereby research projects have separate accounts. However, whereas traditional research budgets were tied to specific grants and any funds not spent at the end of the project would normally revert to the funding body or the parent institution, the new departmental discretionary funds consist principally of surpluses earned by departmental cost centres and are retained by them, usually after some measure of 'taxation' by the parent institution. In one university with several years' experience of financial devolution, net surpluses on earned income are retained by cost centres and may be used for any legitimate purpose including the payment of academic staff salaries or bonuses to staff earning them. Another university, which has a highly centralized system of financial control, treats earned income as a secure basis for regular academic appointments. However, in this case most of the surplus from income generating activities is retained centrally and redistributed as part of the normal allocation procedures: it may or may not go to the cost centres earning the profits, depending on the academic and other priorities of the university.

Discussions, and frequently tensions, between departmental cost centres and central administration usually focus on pricing policy, the allocation of surpluses, the use of departmental discretionary funds and, above all, the staffing of income generating activities.

Staffing issues

The relationship between institutional resource allocation and the incentive structures for individual members of staff is a difficult management issue. Most universities and polytechnics have some system of explicit rewards for established staff who generate external income. There are broadly three approaches. They may be called the 'mainstreaming model', the 'individual incentives model' and the 'small group loyalty model':

1. The mainstreaming model treats external income generation as part of the mainstream activities of the university or polytechnic. All staff are paid according to regular salary scales and any external income is retained centrally and allocated according to institutional priorities regardless of how the income is generated. In return promotion and other career rewards are allocated according to the whole range of contributions that individuals make to the institution, including consultancy earnings. There are two main problems with this approach. One is that a high proportion of staff are at the top of a fixed salary scale with little chance of promotion so for many promotion prospects do not provide a strong incentive. The second is that many academics, especially but not only in universities, still find it difficult to see income generation as a mainstream academic activity.
2. The individual incentives model treats external income generation as peripheral to the legitimate activities of the institution but uses market incentives to reward individuals who make the extra effort to undertake activities which are seen as being in some sense outside their normal responsibilities. Staff retain a significant part of any income they earn but are judged for promotion and other institutional rewards on the basis of performance of traditional academic activities.
3. The third approach takes account of small group loyalties engendered by semi-autonomous departments and centres. Income earned by individuals within these operating units is shared between the institution, the operating unit and the individuals earning it according to formulae that form part of the institution's resource allocation mechanisms.

In none of the case study universities and few of the polytechnics was income generation a major criterion for internal promotion within the principal career grades. It was generally claimed in universities that it is also low on the list of considerations when new appointments from outside are made. However, several university respondents could recall recent appointments, usually at a senior level, where a record of external income generation was an important consideration. The polytechnics were less ambivalent and most respondents agreed that capacity to attract outside earnings is now taken into account in many middle-level as well as senior staff appointments.

If promotion is not influenced by capacity to generate income there need to be direct financial rewards to entrepreneurial individuals. However, even with such incentives there is still widespread resistance from many middle level academic staff against external income generation. A commonly expressed view is that 'if I wanted to be involved in this kind of work, I would be working for a consultancy firm at a much higher salary'. There is, however, a substantial minority of staff, usually in areas such as computing, business studies and engineering who claim to enjoy the challenges of the new financial climate.

However, income generating activities commonly employ staff who do not have established posts. In the case of research this usually means staff with fixed term contracts tied to the funding for the project; in the case of consultancy and short courses it frequently means part-time staff employed on an hourly or daily basis. There are frequently tensions between staff with this kind of contract and those with regular university or polytechnic appointments. The latter believe the non-established staff to be engaged on low level work, and contract staff, who are usually younger, resent what they see as the unjustifiable cushioning of permanent staff who are often unwilling to adapt to changing external circumstances. Such tensions are particularly severe when income-generating activities are concentrated in separate self-financing centres.

Two main reasons are usually given for the establishment of self-financing centres or units. One is to provide a focus for academic activities which interest members of several different departments, and the second is to trigger funds from a specific constituency of support. Until the 1980s most centres were of the first type, but the majority of those established during the past decade are intended to be income generating. The first type can be the means by which old subjects are protected or new subject areas are defined, but the motivating force is academic. In one place staff with a professional interest in philosophy dispersed around several departments have established a centre to provide a focus for their work. Other examples are Women's Studies, and Applied Statistics.

More widespread now are centres which have been established with financial objectives. Some universities have established a large number. In one medium-sized university 17 were reported. It is difficult, however, to form a clear idea of the amount of income they generate. Often their accounts are considered to be part of the income and expenditure of a host department. However, most finance officers believe that at present their income is small and surpluses available to the parent institutions are for the most part negligible.

The employment conditions of the staff of such centres are frequently poor. Until the financial stringency of the 1980s it was normal both in universities and in polytechnics for the great majority of staff carrying out academic work to have permanent contracts with strong employment protection. In the 1970s university academic staff without permanent appointments typically made up less than 20 per cent of the total, and even at the end of the 1970s they had good prospects of obtaining a permanent post in due course. All institutions experienced big increases in the number of non-established staff during the 1980s. In the universities the proportion of full time academic staff paid for from sources other than general university funds rose from 24 per cent in 1981/82 to 35 per cent in 1987/88. Many of these staff are now approaching mid-career, and the prospects of permanent posts become more remote each year.

From the viewpoint of non-established staff the existence of lifetime tenure for established academics may have been an example of the best being the enemy of the good. Although formal tenure did not exist outside the universities, most polytechnic staff in practice had almost equally secure appointments. This meant that temporary staff had to bear the full brunt of financial fluctuations when they occurred and career development policies were almost non-existent. The attraction of this dead-end job for temporary staff was that they expected to find secure academic employment well before they reached the stage of their careers when job mobility becomes difficult.

The changes of the 1980s disrupted this equilibrium. Few new appointments were made to permanent established posts; and the number of people employed on non-established posts increased dramatically. They no longer have the prospect of secure employment within a reasonable period of time. However, they are still treated in many institutions as if they do.

The emergence of an intellectual proletariat has been one of the effects of the funding changes of the 1980s. They have conditions of employment that are often not only worse than their colleagues in established posts, but are also worse than those of people in similar jobs in the private sector. It is, unfortunately, not surprising that a high proportion of individuals on such contracts are women. In 1988/89 45 per cent of staff on 'soft' money of lecturer grade and below were women compared with 15 per cent of staff paid for out of general university funds.

Rigid salary scales and a tendency to under-price contracts have made it difficult to pay any salary premium to compensate for the absence of job security. In some cases this has lowered the quality of recruits, which in turn has seemed to justify the payment of relatively low salaries. Members of staff without permanent employment are usually not deemed to be full academic members of the university or polytechnic. They frequently have no clear representation on the main academic committees and they feel that their interests are rarely taken into account when institutional priorities and strategies are determined. Levies imposed by central institutional authorities on external earnings to meet indirect institutional costs are frequently seen as a device whereby their profits are taken away from them in order to protect the employment of staff with permanent contracts. Many institutions exacerbate the situation by imposing contracts for such staff that not only compare unfavourably with regular university staff but remove much of the job security theoretically guaranteed by employment legislation. Such conditions of employment mean that many temporary staff are more concerned about their next contract than the successful completion of the one they are working on.

Relatively haphazard arrangements for the employment of non-tenured staff have been viable in the past because they were a relatively small proportion of total academic staff employed and were seen as apprenticeships for permanent employment. This situation has changed, especially in several of the areas where significant income generation is possible. It is proving difficult to recruit staff under these employment conditions in such areas as computing, engineering, business studies, statistics, health economics, some branches of chemistry and some foreign languages. One of the most urgent problems facing the management of higher education institutions is to introduce employment and conditions of service that reduce the gaps between established and non-established academic staff.

It is often claimed in universities that there are dangers in providing research staff with permanent employment contracts on the grounds that many research workers are burned out by the time they reach middle age. There is little evidence to support this view. It has certainly been the case in the past that successful research workers have obtained permanent academic posts and, therefore, many of the people remaining in contract research posts in mid-career have not been among the most able. This does not demonstrate, however, that competent research workers cannot remain competent throughout their working lives. Indeed, since most senior university appointments in the past have been made on the basis of research achievement and potential, the original proposition is to some extent a self-contradiction.

University and polytechnic companies

One way of legitimating income generation and reducing the tensions has been the establishment of university and polytechnic companies. Their number has grown very considerably in recent years.

The establishment of limited companies helps to alleviate staffing problems because their employees' terms of employment are separate from the parent institution. Salaries can be determined by market conditions, although in most cases there is some attempt to ensure that they are not too far out of line with academic salaries. However, most academic companies employ only one or two full-time staff, usually managers or administrators. Most of their staff are part time, either on the basis of some kind of secondment from their parent institution or as external consultants to whom work is sub-contracted.

In the belief that there are economies of scale and diversity, all but one of the polytechnics studied had set up umbrella companies to handle all their applied research contracts, consultancies and short course work. Institution-wide companies have advantages in being able to organize interdepartmental and inter-institutional collaboration, and in collaborating with industry and raising capital. They can control quality and pricing policies to maximize the income brought into the polytechnic and 'help us to secure a long term niche in the market'. It is also believed that separate identification of commercial income helps to minimize corporation tax and VAT liabilities.

A separate corporate entity is not, however, generally seen in universities as essential for income generation. Of the 14 universities visited, two had umbrella companies on the polytechnic pattern and one was proposing to establish a university-wide research and consultancy institute as a limited company. Six had no companies formally linked to the university, although in some cases there were small private companies linked to a university department. (It was emphasized in all these cases that the activities of the private companies were kept completely separate from the associated departments.) The remaining five had some small companies, frequently in the area of computer software and biotechnology.

In general university companies have grown up in an *ad hoc* way. There was little explicit concern about tax liabilities, but some finance officers did report some disquiet about becoming involved in venture capital enterprises through associated companies. They worried that 'the Inland Revenue might say it is not the real business of universities to run companies with 75 per cent venture capital. This may be skating on thin ice.' In fact, most university companies are closely linked with the academic work of particular departments, and profit is not always the primary motive. Commercial outlets can provide good experience for students and staff at the 'cutting edge' of technology, and better links with industry can contribute to teaching and research. However, companies that were set up on an *ad hoc* basis are coming under increasing pressure to generate surpluses. Senior managers at one major research-intensive university accepted that its older companies were not profitable to the university because they were set up under relatively lax guidelines, and the Industrial Liaison Office is concerned to see that any new ventures are more profitable.

Administrators at one university expressed doubts about the value of associated companies. They believed that income generating activities can be undertaken just as well by departmental cost centres and that some self-financing centres within departments have been more successful than the university's associated companies. Disadvantages included duplicate administration which could be done more efficiently by the university finance office and the fact that gross earnings were not reported in general university accounts, which 'can be a serious problem when outside earnings are being used as a performance indicator'.

The size of university and polytechnic companies varies a great deal, ranging from a small IT language centre in one college with a few hundred pounds of capital, to a university holding company with five subsidiaries and ten academically led divisions, and an annual turnover of over £6m.

Only two universities out of the fourteen in our sample were able to show significant profits being covenanted back to them from associated companies. In one a separate limited company acts as the clearing office for all income-generating activities and is responsible for all contracts with industry. It started as an academic service unit in 1979, when it played a relatively minor role, but its turnover in 1988 was in excess of £6m. The other university with a profitable umbrella company set up its liaison office as an umbrella company with a number of subdivisions and subsidiaries in 1981. Again, all industrial collaboration and contracts are routed through this company. Senior company managers claimed that this structure ensures good business practice whilst protecting academics from processes that could deflect them from their core activities. By 1988, net profits, which were covenanted back to the university, rose to about £0.6m per year.

At the other extreme there is a very wide variety of small university companies. Small near market companies are often associated with the engineering faculty and are usually based on the research and entrepreneurial skills of individual staff, and the prime movers remain employees of the parent institution. A typical small company in one university was set up to develop and manufacture equipment arising out of the research of the School of Electronic Engineering. Its main products include electrostatic instruments; design, development and manufacture of instrumentation for local power stations, and the designing of a simultaneous translation system with computers. Its annual turnover is about £0.75m.

In another university, a company was established by a psychology lecturer and three postgraduate students in computer science. It markets software and consultancy in the field of artificial intelligence. The university played an active part in setting up the company and continues to be closely involved, essentially by providing support and advice in promoting consultancy contracts and helping to develop software products.

A major area of commercial expansion is continuing education and there are many examples of companies set up to provide training courses for enterprises and local community. Where there is an umbrella company short courses are frequently included as part of its responsibility.

The amount of investment in associated companies by parent institutions also varies, but very few have put in any substantial amount of cash. Some have contributed spare facilities or land, while others see their investment in terms of the loan of seconded staff with the expectation that the company will become self-financing within a limited period.

There are cases where universities and polytechnics are not sole owners of a company but minority shareholders in association with other higher education institutions, private corporations and venture capital companies.

Table 5.1   Trading position of university and polytechnic companies

	Date	Turnover (£)	Gross profit (£)	Net profit before tax (£)	Amount to institution (£)
Polytechnic 1:					
Poly Services Ltd.	1988/89	250,000	–	–	–
Poly Services Ltd.	1987/88	176,408	93,406	37,221	–
Poly Services Ltd.	1986/87	109.104	34,326	10,361	–
University 1:					
Commercial activities	1987/88	148,818	–	–	–
UNI Ltd.	1987/88	205,152	–	37,796	–
UNI Ltd.	1986/87	307,358	–	109,889	–
University 2:					
Mos Ltd.	1987/88	79,846	8,885	–	5,931
Fund Ltd.	1986/87	70,500	7,010	–	54,845
Technologies Ltd.	1986/87	332,901	57,231	2,386	–
University 3:					
Enterprises Ltd.	1987/88	183,810	19,191	3,660	–
University 4:					
Energy Co. Ltd.	1987/88	1,756,000	–	108,000	105,000
Polytechnic 2:					
Business Services	1987/88	6,578,600	891,180	364,244	200,000
Polytechnic 3:					
Polytechnic Products Ltd.	1987/88	169,603	99,881	45,362	–
Polytechnic 4:					
Polytechnic International	1985/86	207,229	44,084	13,881	15,370

Source: Institutional Survey. (Pseudonyms have been used for company names.)

There are also many examples of three-way companies, set up by individual academics. There is no single pattern, but usually an individual staff member or research group develops ideas, the institution provides the research facilities and outside interests provide financial backing. One university has several small companies that are being developed by academic staff in areas like biology and computing. The university has minority holdings and some staff, in addition to the founders, also have personal stakes. One company rents university facilities and is financed by outside venture capital. The two directors are academics who are paid part-time by the company. The university hopes that it will eventually receive dividends from its share capital, but at the moment profits are invested in equipment and development. Senior managers at one institution are so enthusiastic about investing in new academic ventures, that they are contributing personal venture capital in some cases.

A key feature of polytechnic and university companies is that dividends are covenanted back to the parent institution. Once profits have been declared there is a variety of arrangements for distributing them within the parent institution. One polytechnic holding company returns 80 per cent of any surplus to the unit that generated the income, and retains 20 per cent for the parent institution. The 80 per cent is divided between the department and individual staff members involved. In another model, an umbrella company handling all contracts for a university retains control over profits produced by its academically led subdivisions, in which academic staff act as non-executive directors supported by operational managers and staff employed directly by the umbrella company. Directors' fees provide financial incentives to individuals. In addition the company pays departments directly for the use of their equipment and facilities. Profits revert to the university's central management, which distributes them through its research and teaching committees.

Table 5.1 shows the trading position of a sample of companies in the case study universities and polytechnics during the 1980s. It illustrates the small scale of the great majority of these companies.

The contributions received from a subsidiary company are not always in the form of cash. Equipment obtained to fulfil a company contract may become available for teaching and academic research. At one university, a head of department claimed that there was an incentive to take profits on contracts in the form of equipment, because 'otherwise the central administration would retain an excessive amount as overheads'.

The small scale of activity has some advantages for the parent institution. There are worries about associated companies becoming too successful and becoming directly competitive with the university or polytechnic itself. There are some examples of companies that have broken away from the parent institution when they began to make serious money.

Science and technology parks

The growth of small companies tied to particular research groups may be facilitated by the proximity of a science or technology park.

The science park, a planned development of high-technology enterprises in an attractive physical environment with close links to a university, is the most ambitious and highly organized of the forms of external income generation and collaboration between industry and higher education that developed during the 1980s. It has received great publicity as a concept and many hopes are pinned upon it as a mechanism of technology transfer as well as a source of income for higher education. Many universities and a few polytechnics are developing one.

Several types of science park can be distinguished. In academic terms the purest is the research park sited on or close to the campus. The main activity is applied research, often in liaison with industry, but based on the university or polytechnic's own research. Typically, the academic institution retains the dominant role in the management of this kind of park with scientific advance and technology transfer being of at least equal significance to the income generated from rents.

In the more general science park product development is as significant as research. The role of industrial partners becomes more important. Prototype production facilities often exist but the creation of a climate of collaboration between scientists and engineers in industry and those in higher education remains important, though direct income generation for the higher education institution is often the primary concern.

Both these types of science park have tended to develop, as a result of spontaneous initiatives rather than as a part of conscious development strategies. A third variety, more accurately described as a technology park, is typically a commercial development on university or polytechnic land to accommodate companies engaged in the commercial application of high technology. Academic involvement is often low and there may be a substantial element of production, sales and servicing work. A further step in the direction of pure commercialization occurs when the technology park develops into a business park where research and development are relatively unimportant and the site is in reality little more than an attractive industrial estate.

Science and research parks provide a mechanism through which university and polytechnic companies can evolve. They enable technological knowledge to be transferred both ways between academia and industry. They allow the academic community to maintain contact with commercial realities and, their advocates claim, encourage the development of a culture in which academia and business can generate further collaboration in teaching, research and enterprise.

The Cambridge and Heriot-Watt parks were the pioneers in this country and their success, encouraged others to follow suit. A stimulus came in the 1980s when cuts in higher education funding forced universities to look for new opportunities and changes in Treasury rules about generating income from university land permitted them to do so. Another more positive factor was a readiness on the part of venture capitalists to go into academically related technology, in part attracted by funds provided through the Alvey programme and other government schemes to encourage technology transfer.

The pressure to make full use of science park facilities has, in some cases, led to dilution of the original concept and their evolution into more general business parks: in some developments at the end of the 1980s speculative building was a prominent feature followed, as boom gave way to recession in the 1990s, by problems of under-utilization.

Five of the case study universities visited, but only one of the polytechnics had science and technology parks at various stages of development, and two others were planned. In one of these the Vice-Chancellor explained why the University Council had just taken the decision to establish a science park. They believe commercial tenants will maintain close relations with research in the university, and that the park will act as a focal point to attract new high-technology industry to a region where there is little industry: and eventually the university will receive a financial return.

The university's contribution will be in the form of land and equity investment of £100,000. The local County Council has promised a loan but most of the capital must come from the financial markets. The university will retain the freehold of the land, giving a 30-year lease to its own management company. The Bursar described how a Working Group, which is chaired by the Chairman of a large multi-national company, is looking for major institutional investors. The management company aims to retain a majority shareholding or at least a 'golden share' with partners from the funding consortium. The university believes it is necessary for it to control tenancies to ensure that they are compatible with the university's objectives. It aims to adhere to a 'Cambridge-style definition of science park – not an office complex'. It was claimed that 'there would not be much point in doing it if there is no cross-fertilization between university and industry'.

Other universities also were conscious of the charge that they were more concerned with making money than with research and technology transfer. At one, a science park had been developed with the backing of three local authorities and private investors. It has been successful in that it has grown fast and now accommodates 30 or 40 companies. Senior administrators claim that the university has been careful to select companies which have the potential to contribute to at least one of its departments. In this they consider that the university differs from many others 'where the Science Parks are little more then property leasing operations'. However, the university management realizes that 'the companies on the Park will use the university if it is in their interest to do so but they will be equally willing to call on expertise elsewhere'.

In one university the local City Council is putting in a major bid to the EC for funds which includes 'a research hotel' on the university science park. This would be a multi-purpose and multi-disciplinary science and research facility with shared support facilities rented to academics and academic based enterprises for relatively short periods during the lifetime of particular projects. It would permit experimentation with new ideas without the need to undertake the infrastructural investment that is similar for most high-technology enterprises (telephone system, fax machine, reception facilities, wiring for computer networks, suitably equipped laboratories and workshops etc.). The idea is an interesting approach to the problem of filling the gap between fundamental research in the laboratory and large scale commercial exploitation.

Some other institutions were less reticent about their reasons for embarking on science park developments. In one university where senior management staff declared themselves to be 'much more keen on recognizing relevant and income generating activities' than they used to be, there is a 'Field Study area' of 300 acres of green belt which is now, in addition, a science park. This earns £175,000 per year in rent and is believed to be 'influential in promoting contract work'.

Another university was fortunate in owning 70 acres of nearby land, which is extremely convenient for road, air and rail transport. The land was purchased by the University Trust Fund which was set up as a result of a national appeal when the University was founded in the 1960s. Planning permission was obtained in 1983 and building work started in 1984.

The objectives of this Research Park are stated to be:

  (i) to further extend the University's interaction with research and development scientists and engineers in industry;
 (ii) to create a centre of research, development and technical excellence linked with a major British Technological University;
(iii) to create some independent income for the University so that it may continue to develop its own research, technical and educational base without some of the constraints imposed by the method of central resource distribution to Universities.

The dominance of the third objective is shown by the agreement that the initial stage of development depended on the achievement of three goals:

  (i) to find an 'anchor tenant', who would be willing to lease a major building in the park and develop facilities for research and development;
 (ii) to find a company to launch and manage an innovation centre;
(iii) to find a number of high-technology companies to be tenants for smaller units.

The 'anchor tenant' has taken the largest building on the Research Park as its Development and Executive Centre which now houses 300 technical, scientific and management staff. This tenant paid £2.5m, which was invested in new buildings. More recently a subsidiary of the company has moved to the Park. The presence of the company on the Research Park is an asset to both the company and the students at the University and it recruits a number of the university's graduates each year. There have been a number of research links with the Department of Chemical Engineering, and the Head of that Department reported that contact with the company is frequent and very often informal – they often supply the university with useful materials and the university can help the company by responding to individual queries or research enquiries.

There were, by the end of 1988, 45 tenants in the Research Park and work had begun on a further phase of its development. £9m had been invested by the University in buildings and facilities and the Research Park has earned £1.5m in rent. By 1992 the university is expecting to earn £1.5m a year in rents alone. It has invested income from the Research Park in further developments and has borrowed on the security of existing buildings. It has leased land to a major hotel chain for a new prestige executive oriented hotel which, it is claimed, has increased the attractiveness of the site to companies.

The Marketing Director attributes this success to several factors:

(a)   The site was magnificent, close to major motorways, excellent links to airports, and good rail services to the rest of the country.

(b)   The University took the decision to run the Research Park itself, so that management is *by* the university *for* the university. This 'has proved to be much better than selling the Research Park to a Property Developer or Pension Fund'.

(c)   The university has always had close links with industry, and therefore 'understands what modern high-tech companies want'.

(d)   The university has always done careful market research.

(e)   It has been extremely careful about what is built on the site, to ensure high quality.

(f)   It has been innovative and flexible in the type of leasing arrangements offered, which range from 6 to 125 years. This makes it attractive to new, small companies which are willing to lease small units for 6 years.

(g)   The Vice-Chancellor has been strongly committed from the beginning.

Even in this commercially successful venture it was believed to be important to emphasize organic links with the university where they existed. 'At least 8 of the 45 tenant companies have been set up by university academics to exploit ideas or inventions arising from research at the University.' Other companies have developed collaborative research projects with the university and their staff act as visiting teachers and advisers. Many companies in the Research Park offer industrial experience to undergraduates during their industrial placements, and also employ graduates from the university. These are all important benefits to the university, in addition to companies offering consultancies to academic staff, increasing conference business and generally 'raising the profile of the University'.

Despite these success stories and high hopes, the commercial and academic success of Science Parks as a whole remains unproven. With few exceptions the direct financial returns to academic institutions from commercial exploitation of research are limited and there are relatively few research contracts from tenant firms. The main source of profit is in the return from the rental and thus differ little in principle from the income from rents received by Oxford and Cambridge Colleges for several hundred years. The majority of Science Parks have yet to declare a profit and have taken the decision to reinvest any surplus in the growth of the company.

The 'anchor tenant' is an important constituent of the commercially oriented Science Park. We found several instances where universities employed agents to find the 'anchor tenant' and sometimes also to find tenants for smaller units. Several referred to market research which shows that companies like the concept of a 'high-tech village' with good facilities in a pleasant environment. Science Parks often have plenty of space, lakes and trees and many have employed landscape gardeners to create a 'user friendly' environment as well as 'high-tech' facilities.

Some early parks with a firm base in a university have grown steadily over a period of years to achieve an established reputation and commercial viability. Other more recent developments appear to have unrealistic expectations based on the early success stories. Some ventures were started in haste in order to take advantage of what was thought to be a lucrative new growth area at a time of rapid economic expansion but severe cutbacks in government academic funding. Difficulties have occurred when a Science Park is sited some distance away from the university as this reduces opportunities for interaction between the universities and the companies using the Park. Some have suffered from tensions between property speculators, the host university and other partners, with considerable pressure to fill the industrial units available for rent without full consideration of the best needs of the university.

One manager of a commercially successful science park summarized the prerequisites of success thus: 'If universities are to become commercial operators they must have successful commercial-style management and be prepared to "think greedy", which academics often do not like.' However, there is much evidence that university and polytechnic managers in their approach to income generation in general, and not just the creation of science parks, have learned to think greedy since 1980. Whether this will in the long run benefit British higher education is not yet proved.

6

The Development of an
Overseas Student Market*

The introduction of full-cost fees

Until 1980, overseas students in Britain were heavily subsidized out of public funds in much the same way as home students though at a somewhat lower rate. Fees well above the home student rate were introduced in 1967, but they remained considerably below average cost per student. The number of overseas students rose sharply during the 1970s, and by 1979 the cost of subsidizing them was over £100m. In November 1979 the government announced that from October 1980 all newly registered overseas students would be expected to pay fees which covered the average costs of their courses, and the subsidy to institutions would be withdrawn over a 3-year period, so that by 1983 all students who were domiciled outside the European Community would be paying full-cost fees.

This announcement caused fierce controversy. Universities and polytechnics predicted a dramatic fall in the number of overseas students and hence in their income. There was debate about Britain's obligations to developing countries, particularly in the Commonwealth. Many commentators emphasized the educational, political and commercial benefits derived from the presence in Britain of students from abroad, and some foreign governments protested about the sudden imposition of full-cost fees when other European countries continued to subsidize all students in higher education, regardless of nationality or domicile.

The increase in fees was indeed followed by a sharp fall in the number of overseas students coming to Britain. Between 1979 and 1983, their number in universities, polytechnics and colleges fell by 28 per cent, from 61 to 48 thousand. In 1983 the government announced an increase in funding under the so-called 'Pym Package' which increased scholarships by £46m, over 3 years. A new programme of Foreign and Commonwealth Office scholarships was introduced, special support was provided for students from Malaysia, Hong Kong and Cyprus and there was an increase in

* This chapter was written in collaboration with Maureen Woodhall

scholarships for research students under the Overseas Research Students Award Scheme. Since 1983 the main features of British policy towards overseas students have remained largely unchanged. By the mid-1980s there was, in place of the previous indiscriminate subsidy of all overseas students, a policy of full-cost fees, combined with targeted scholarships for particular categories of students, or those from particular countries.

When full-cost fees were first introduced in 1980, the DES recommended minimum fees for overseas students in universities, of £2,000 for Arts, Humanities and Social Science, £3,000 for Science and Engineering and £5,000 for Medicine; in polytechnics and colleges the recommended minimum fees were £2,400 for classroom-based courses and £3,300 for laboratory-based courses. Subsequently the UGC and the Council of Local Education Authorities (CLEA) recommended minimum fee levels each year. Although the government announced, in the 1985 Green Paper that 'it is for institutions and local authorities to determine the actual fees to be charged in the light of their own circumstances' in practice most institutions continued to charge the 'recommended' fee, but from 1989 the force of these recommendations has been considerably reduced. The Committee of Vice-Chancellors and Principals (CVCP) took over responsibility for fee recommendations for universities (which was formerly the responsibility of the UGC) and the Committee of Directors of Polytechnics (CDP) provided guidelines for polytechnics in 1989, but since 1990 no recommended fee levels have been set for polytechnics. However, the CVCP indicated that its proposals were only a 'mild form of recommended retail price' and stated 'if universities wish to set lower or higher prices they are free to do so' (THES 30 December, 1988, p. 4).

The introduction of full-cost fees, and the subsequent developments, including the gradual relaxation of 'price controls' in the form of regulations setting minimum or recommended fees, and the shift towards selective subsidies, through targeted scholarship programmes for selected overseas students, meant that the 1980s saw the emergence and development of an explicit market in higher education for overseas students. The size of this market has been influenced by government policies, the marketing activities of universities and polytechnics, exchange rates, which determine the relative price of higher education in Britain compared with other countries, and the growth of international competition as other receiving countries, such as USA, Australia and Japan, have tried to increase their share of the market.

This chapter examines the development of the overseas student market in publicly funded higher education in the 1980s, and considers how the decline in overseas student numbers, which followed the introduction of full-cost fees in 1980, was reversed after 1983, when numbers again began to increase, until, by 1989/90, the total number of overseas students in higher education was 71,000, which was 16 per cent higher than when full-cost fees were introduced. The increase for universities alone was over 26 per cent.

Government policy and national marketing

A statement of government policy was set out in a review of Government support for overseas students in 1989.

In 1988/89 the Government provided more than £110m to support more than 22,000 students from overseas. These resources have been deployed through a range of targeted schemes each designed to serve specific objectives within the Government's overall aim of bringing more overseas students to Britain. These objectives are:

Win influential friends overseas by enabling future leaders, decision makers and opinion formers from all walks of life to study in the UK;

Help the development of manpower skills and resources in developing countries;

Promote the security and prosperity of the UK by cultivating good political and commercial relations with other countries;

Ensure a continued supply of world class research students in UK universities.

(Round Table, 1989, p. 1)

In addition to scholarships and awards, the Government provides nearly £1m per year for various organizations and programmes which provide support, guidance and accommodation advice for overseas students, including UKCOSA and voluntary organizations such as HOST, which organizes hospitality for overseas students in vacations. The purpose of this funding is 'to help ensure that overseas students who come to Britain are well received and enjoy maximum benefit from their stay' (Round Table, 1989, p. 2).

The overall aim of such measures is thus to help attract overseas students to Britain in order to achieve specific objectives associated with British interests, including foreign policy, trade, aid to developing countries and high-quality research. The Government justifies this policy of targeted support as being more cost-effective than a policy of 'haphazard and indiscriminate subsidies which were not being directed to serve the aims of British policy at all closely' (Renton, 1985).

The success of this policy depends in large part on successful marketing. The Pym Package included £100,000 a year for the British Council to help with the promotion of British higher education abroad including the establishment of the British Council Education Counselling Service (ECS) in 1984, which aims to publicize opportunities in British higher education and to inform UK institutions about recruitment opportunities. The ECS is now funded through subscriptions from the universities, polytechnics and colleges which choose to become members. Membership in 1989 comprised some 90 institutions, including all but three universities and one polytechnic. Initially ECS set up offices in Hong Kong, Malaysia and

Singapore, but its activities have since been extended to include Brunei, Cyprus, Japan, Korea and it was planned to open small offices in four or five additional countries in 1990/91.

The British Council stresses that the ECS is essentially a partnership. It acts rather like an Export Trade Association, to provide opportunities for its members to carry out effective promotional activities. It organizes British Higher Education Fairs and distributes publicity materials and carries out market research on the demand for higher education in particular countries. In its first few years ECS also ran a placement service and provided counselling for potential students, but it has gradually moved to a greater emphasis on promotional activities and has abandoned the individual placement service in the belief that it was in danger of duplicating the work of the Universities Central Council on Admissions (UCCA) and the Polytechnics Central Admission System (PCAS). It continues to provide advice and training for educational counsellors in sending countries, but the main focus is on publicity and on facilitating institutions' own recruitment efforts.

Marketing by universities

The Institute of Education carried out surveys of overseas students in 1980 and 1985, to examine the implications of full-cost fees, for students and for institutional policies and practice. The report of the 1985 survey concluded that 'the most noticeable finding . . . is the considerable amount of entrepreneurial activity . . . most universities now rely on overseas students for between 5 and 16 per cent of their income. Since 1980 more than half the universities have introduced internal incentive schemes to encourage and reward departments for the recruitment of overseas fee-paying students and we found numerous instances of new courses being created and new recruitment initiatives.' (Williams, Woodhall and O'Brien, 1986, pp. 5–8). More than half of the universities had established a committee to co-ordinate overseas student recruitment efforts and a third had appointed a recruitment officer, either full or part-time. The study noted that 'the public sector has been much less entrepreneurial', partly because many institutions had no financial incentive to increase overseas recruitment, and partly because of the pressure of demand from home students between 1980 and 1985, although 'the situation is now changing and a number of polytechnics in particular are beginning to take active steps to recruit students from overseas' (Williams *et al.*, 1986, p. 5).

Although there was evidence of considerable diversity of views both within and between institutions, the authors concluded that 'undoubtedly finance is now the main factor motivating the recruitment efforts of most universities and some polytechnics'. The successive cuts in funding that occurred between 1980 and 1984 meant that by the time of the survey 'the financial motive behind overseas enrolment is now very strong and most universities have made determined efforts to restore income lost as a result of the withdrawal of subsidy in 1980' (Williams *et al.* 1986, p. 61). These efforts included an increase in marketing overseas, the development of links with institutions abroad, membership of the British Council's Education Counselling Service (ECS) and in a few cases universities employed agents to recruit overseas.

Polytechnics were less involved in recruitment activities in 1985. Fewer than half had any central policy on overseas student recruitment, and:

> most polytechnics have been preoccupied with a substantial rise in home demand which has more than offset falling overseas numbers. The requirements of NAB and tighter funding have further limited the capacity of polytechnics to take action on overseas intake and their interest in doing so. There are now clear signs, however, that some have begun to establish recruitment and welfare policies and there is a general burgeoning interest in the financial benefits of maintaining and increasing an overseas student presence.
>
> (Williams *et al.*, 1986, p. 73)

A major review of policy towards overseas students was published by the Overseas Students Trust (OST) in 1987. This draws upon the findings of the 1985 survey, as well as an analysis of national trends both in Britain and abroad. Noting the 'significant increases in the resources devoted to marketing and promotional activities by most universities, rather fewer polytechnics and a scattering of other further education institutions', the OST observes that 'as long as due consideration is given to their responsibilities towards the students recruited, the expansion of such entrepreneurship is to be welcomed and encouraged' (OST, 1987, p. 38). The OST concludes that the increased concentration on recruitment of overseas students has had positive consequences, since 'it has caused some institutions, if only in terms of commercial concern with "after-sales care", to look afresh at the suitability of their courses and modes of instruction, and the adequacy of their accommodation and other pastoral arrangements' (OST, 1987, p. 37).

The increase in marketing and recruitment activities in universities, noted in the 1985 study, has been maintained and indeed intensified in most of the 14 universities and university colleges visited in 1989. Ten have an overseas student recruitment or liaison officer and most have established an international office and a committee dealing specifically with overseas recruitment. In most cases there is a single individual with overall responsibility for co-ordinating recruitment activities of departments, or a small committee which carries out this function, but in five there is an International Office with several staff and a specific budget for recruitment visits abroad. In two of the 14 universities overseas recruitment was part of the general responsibility of the Admissions Office, and no special appointment of an overseas student recruitment officer had been made, although in both cases there was active discussion, about ways of increasing overseas enrolments. Several universities had produced reports on over-seas student recruitment, which formulated or recommended an overall policy and in some cases established targets for each department. All the universities were members of the British Council's Educational Coun-selling Service, and in addition several were members of consortia, such as the Northern Consortium, set up specifically to market higher education institutions in the North of England and to negotiate with foreign govern-ments and institutions.

All the case study universities send academic staff abroad, either specially for recruitment, or with some responsibility for recruitment in addition to other academic business. In addition to universal advertising through brochures, several had organized special visits by Overseas Re-cruitment Officers to particular countries (notably USA and several coun-tries in South East Asia) and some had established links with institutions overseas which had, at least in part, the aim of stimulating recruitment, particularly of postgraduate students. Only in a few cases did universities report the employment of overseas agents, although in certain countries, notably Japan, it was thought to be cost-effective by some respondents.

Several universities reported that they now employ a more intensive and a more professional approach than in the early 1980s. One, which has increased the number of overseas students by 50 per cent since 1981 re-ported that initially it had relied on academics to recruit students during their visits abroad for research or other academic purposes, but 'the re-sults were hopeless', and an International Office has now been estab-lished, which employs several staff, including a full-time officer in Hong Kong, responsible for recruitment and for organizing 'split-site' courses.

Very few universities were able to estimate the total cost of their over-seas recruitment activities, but those that had established an International Office usually had a specific budget for overseas visits and other market-ing or recruitment activities. At the time of the 1985 survey we estimated that on average expenditure on overseas recruitment in 1984/85 was £16,000 per university; this figure included the cost of travel abroad, pub-licity, and membership of the British Council's Educational Counselling Service, but not the costs of staff time or overheads. The 1989 survey re-vealed considerable variation among those universities able to provide de-tailed figures. One which receives about 5 per cent of its income from overseas students has an International Office with a budget of £250,000. Another spends between £60,000 and £100,000 a year on overseas re-cruitment, and receives an annual income of over £2.5m from overseas student fees.

There were many examples of new courses that had been developed for the overseas market. There has been an enormous expansion of 1-year Master's and diploma level courses, for the very large numbers who prefer a 1-year course to a longer postgraduate research programme. There has been a significant increase in many universities in the number of American students taking 'Junior Year Abroad' courses, for which they gain credit towards a degree from their own universities. Although not now considered as 'overseas' students, there has also been a significant increase in the number of European students coming to Britain for a term or longer as part of a degree course in their own university. Some, but by no means all of these, were sponsored by the European Community ERASMUS scheme.

Until recently there was little information about students who are in Britain for a short period as part of a degree course elsewhere. Since they are not studying for a British qualification and are not in Britain for a full academic year, they may not appear in the regular statistics of overseas students. The 1985 survey found that many universities reported an increase in overseas students, particularly from USA, studying for a short period in Britain as part of their degree course in their own universities. The majority come from the USA or from the EC, and most students were studying languages, humanities, social studies or a multi-disciplinary course. Eleven of the 14 case study universities had American students on Junior Year Abroad (JYA) programmes, and several believe that this is an important and growing market. One university reported a significant increase in the number of Americans coming for one term rather than a year.

Some universities devote considerable time to building strong links with American institutions, and there were other examples of institutional links in Asia, and one or two in other regions, including Eastern Europe, Scandinavia and the Middle East. There were examples of 'split-site' courses in Hong Kong and Malaysia, and some universities had established co-operative arrangements with other UK institutions and consortia, to provide such courses. Four of the 14 universities have established links with British further education institutions, which provide 'access' or 'foundation' courses for overseas students, before they proceed to degree-level courses, and another university in the study was actively exploring this possibility.

There has also been a significant increase in the provision of short courses for overseas students, particularly from Europe, including Eastern Europe as well as the EC, and several universities intend to increase their provision in this area, believing that ERASMUS and the creation of a single European market in 1992 will provide an important stimulus for short periods of study in this country.

Several universities reported increased provision of English language courses. More than half offer both pre-sessional English courses and remedial language classes and one, which runs an English Language Institute, gives all overseas students a language proficiency test on arrival, and on the basis of this test about a half are judged to be in need of some language support.

Welfare provision is usually the responsibility of the Overseas Student Office or International Office, but in some cases an officer has been appointed, with particular responsibility for overseas student welfare. Several universities reported an increase in time devoted to this activity. In most cases it included help with accommodation, immigration problems, and advice for students facing financial hardships and personal problems, but a few go considerably further and one Welfare Officer organized trips for overseas students in the vacation, and arranged visits to English families at Christmas, as well as providing general pastoral advice and orientation courses.

A vital aspect of welfare emphasized in many universities is the provision of accommodation. A recent survey revealed a shortage of suitable accommodation in many areas. The report (OST, 1990) highlights the importance of adequate accommodation as 'a vital element in the total package offered by responsible recruiters' and warns that adverse publicity about an 'accommodation crisis' in some areas 'rang alarm bells among those considering study in Britain'. A shortage of suitable accommodation for students who are often older than their British counterparts and may wish to bring their families was mentioned by several overseas student advisers as one of the most important factors limiting future growth of recruitment. Some universities try to guarantee accommodation for overseas students, at least in their first year, but this is not always possible, particularly for those who arrive after the start of the academic year; it may also sometimes be a cause of resentment among British students. The problem is particularly severe in London and the South East, and in more than one institution in this area fears were expressed that the shortage of accommodation and high cost of living in London will seriously reduce their chances of increasing overseas recruitment.

In a few cases universities have negotiated special contracts for groups of overseas students. These contracts may be with a particular institution, for example American universities sending groups of Junior Year Abroad (JYA) students, or with foreign governments sending students with specific training needs. Some contracts involve special 'discounts' on fees for a group of students. Such special arrangements are not yet widespread, but there is some evidence that the American JYA market is becoming particularly competitive and there is increasing pressure for 'price deals'. Some universities have consciously rejected such a policy but, while the case studies did not suggest that a 'price war' is in prospect, several informants spoke of 'a greater willingness to show flexibility' in setting fees. In a few cases this means charging fees that are *higher*, rather than *lower* than those for similar courses in other universities, but there is not much enthusiasm for charging overseas students 'what the market will bear', because, it is believed, this would discriminate against students of high ability but limited income. In a few cases additional fees are charged for practical or laboratory work, when this imposes particularly high costs or sometimes, it seems, when it is believed that particular students are able and willing to pay them.

An interesting example of a contract negotiated by a group of institutions, which will cover a substantial number of Malaysian students following 'split-site' courses, is the agreement between the Northern

Consortium, which represents 12 institutions in the North of England (including both universities and polytechnics) and the Malaysian government. This contract, worth £14m in total, is bringing 2,800 Malaysian students to Britain over 3 years; these students spend the first year of their courses studying in Malaysia, followed by study in Britain. This deal is regarded as a serious blow by some institutions in other regions which now feel severely disadvantaged in trying to recruit in Malaysia.

All the universities in the sample had increased their income from overseas student fees since 1985, in some cases substantially. The average increase between 1985 and 1988 was 25 per cent but in one it was 78 per cent and in another 62 per cent. Since 1980 four had seen this source of income double and another four of the 14 had increased it by over 50 per cent.

Most universities offer financial incentives to departments to increase their recruitment of overseas students. In some cases the departmental funding formulae allow departments to keep a proportion of the overseas student fee income, but the proportions vary from 10 per cent to 66 per cent. In a few cases departments have used this extra income to pay for additional staff, but in most it was used for non-staff expenditure.

Polytechnics and colleges

In 1985, there was less entrepreneurial activity in the polytechnics and colleges than in the universities, but by 1989 this was changing. Among the ten case study institutions in the polytechnic and colleges sector, four had set up an International Office by 1989.

All polytechnics experienced substantial reductions in overseas student numbers, following the introduction of full-cost fees. Three of the case study institutions reported that numbers had fallen by over 50 per cent since 1981, and most had continued to experience a decline after 1984, when numbers in universities began to increase. However, of the ten non-university institutions visited one polytechnic in the North and one college in the South-East reported considerable increases since 1984, including in one case a substantial increase in American JYA students.

Seven of the eight polytechnics reported an increase in marketing effort since 1988 but a senior administrator in one in the South East of England thought 'that polytechnics on the whole are losing overseas students as more and more universities compete for them'. This institution has recently agreed a policy on overseas student recruitment strategies, which is far more detailed than that of any other polytechnic or college visited, and more detailed than many of the universities. The aim is to double the proportion of overseas students from 6 per cent to between 10 and 15 per cent by 1991/92. The strategy is based on the concept of 'responsible recruitment', which aims to provide high quality provision for overseas students. The main elements of this strategy are:

1. Increasing recruitment in existing markets and exploring new markets. Expenditure on overseas marketing increased from £28,000 in 1984/85 to £105,000 in 1988/89.
2. Increasing the supply of accommodation: 'staff who have recruited overseas have learned that the single most important demand of overseas students is for guaranteed accommodation'.
3. Increased financial support for overseas students, together with a greater willingness to guarantee a fee level for the duration of a course: 'In setting fees for overseas students, the Finance Director should be prepared to predict the level for the duration of a student's course'.
4. Increased support services, including both welfare and language support.
5. Development of split-site and foundation or access courses.
6. Increased recruitment to short study abroad schemes, as a result of greater modularization of courses.
7. Increased marketing overseas, through British Council and other initiatives.
8. Developing faculty incentives: 'the creative energy within faculties must be harnessed to encourage new and innovative ways of recruiting overseas students, within the framework of responsible recruitment'.

This was the most explicit strategy statement that we encountered in any institution. There were, however, other signs that polytechnics and colleges were adopting more active policies than in 1985. Several had negotiated contracts with foreign governments or institutions. These included American JYA programmes in two cases, contracts with colleges in Thailand, a summer school for Italian students, a course for Malaysian students in Business Studies, and a few contracts with Middle East governments. In two cases polytechnics had joined a consortium marketing a group of institutions. Two polytechnics were also developing financial incentive schemes for departments that increased their recruitment of overseas students, but such schemes were less widespread than in universities, reflecting the smaller amount of financial devolution to departments in this sector.

The emergence of the concept of responsible recruitment

The last 10 years have seen the emergence of the 'overseas student market' as a significant policy issue in British higher education. It is becoming an increasingly competitive market and there are frequent references to 'cut-throat competition' with regard to recruitment in Hong Kong, Malaysia and some other countries. Having embarked on active recruitment policies more recently than universities, polytechnics and colleges often set even more ambitious targets for future growth. Although claims of a price war are vehemently denied, there are instances of institutions varying fee levels to maximize income, and a few references to setting them according to 'what the market will bear'.

The market is seen to be increasingly competitive at the international level as well as in the UK, with both Australia and Japan making particular efforts to increase recruitment from South-East Asia. The response has been an increase in promotional activities, both on the part of individual institutions and collectively through activities such as the ECS and the Northern Consortium. Many new courses have been designed especially for the overseas market, including special short courses for 'Junior Year Abroad' programmes, language courses, access courses linked with degree programmes and 'split-site' degree courses.

The financial gains are obvious, with several of the case study universities reporting significant increases in income from overseas student fees. But there are also frequent references to academic benefits to British students from an overseas student presence. How much of this is self-deluding rhetoric it is not possible to say. There have been some protests from overseas students that they are valued for the fees they pay rather than for any educational benefits they bring, and increased awareness of the importance of overseas students has been accompanied in some quarters by a fear that they may be exploited.

In the light of such pressures a theme that is appearing in many institutional policy statements is the need for responsible recruitment policies. In the case study institutions we were told about examples of a 'hard-sell' approach (always in *other* institutions), but the notion of responsible recruitment, which has been strongly urged by UKCOSA, was stressed many times. A policy document in one polytechnic recognized that:

> the Polytechnic must put into practice the principles of responsible recruitment if it is to compete in today's highly competitive overseas student market. Overseas student recruitment involves giving (services, accommodation, English language tuition, scholarships, etc.) as well as taking full-cost fees.

A similar message was found in a policy document in another polytechnic.

> If we are to attract overseas students to our polytechnic we will need to look carefully at what is on offer both to ensure that the general education provision is appropriate and that we are accepting and fulfilling our responsibility to these students as for all others. This is more important perhaps since these students are expected to pay full-cost fees.

The fact that both these statements come from the polytechnics is significant, not because such sentiments are uncommon in universities, but because polytechnics are more likely to have formulated recent explicit policy statements. In general there are signs of an increased awareness of the importance of measures to safeguard the quality of the educational experience of students while they are here – in terms of language and study skills courses, counselling services and other welfare provision.

There is also growing recognition of the need to be professional in recruitment and publicity. Not only were many institutions becoming more active in recruitment, they also felt they were learning how to make their recruitment efforts more effective. There are mixed reactions to the contribution of the Educational Counselling Service. Virtually all the case study institutions were members, the only exception being a college with hardly any overseas students. In some institutions it was believed that this represents good value for money, whereas others were more sceptical about its value for individual institutions. One informant expressed this strongly: 'It is doing a good job for British Higher Education in general, but not a lot for an individual university', while in another university it was claimed that the ECS sometimes acts as a 'monopolistic agent for providers of British higher education', and thus discourages initiative by individual institutions. The ECS stresses that it does not offer an individual placement service. Its aim is to complement the efforts of individual institutions, and it must respond to the needs of all its members rather than promoting individual institutions.

Clearly there have been significant changes in recruitment strategies, the development of new courses geared specifically for the overseas market and, perhaps most importantly, a change in attitudes towards overseas students as customers in many institutions. Many of the changes are welcomed by those members of universities, polytechnics and colleges who believe that higher education should have an international element and that there are significant educational, as well as financial benefits from the presence of overseas students. Others are alarmed by the fact that universities are being awarded Queen's Awards for Exports, and fear that commercial, rather than academic criteria are being applied to recruitment. There is a danger that overseas students may feel exploited, and believe that they are valued for the fee income they bring rather than their intellectual and academic contributions. On the other hand, there is clear evidence that overseas students are often better treated now than before the introduction of full-cost fees, because they are paying customers. There is also evidence of a change in attitude by some overseas students themselves. The recent OST survey of overseas student housing needs and expectations stressed 'No longer do overseas students themselves think of their places at British universities or polytechnics as favours conferred: instead they talk in terms of value for money' (OST, 1990).

Many universities and polytechnics are trying to formulate a policy on the appropriate balance between home and overseas students. We found a wide variety of views, with some polytechnics and universities setting 5 per cent as a target for the proportion of overseas students, fears in one university department that the current proportion of 25 per cent is too high, and 20 per cent would represent a better balance, while in several other universities a figure of 10 to 15 per cent is thought to be 'about right'. Such questions are likely to generate further debate in the future. There is no right answer, but it is noteworthy that the introduction of full-cost fees and the response of institutions to this change, have thrown the questions into sharper focus.

The shift in government policy towards targeted, rather than general, financial support has also focused greater attention on the criteria for awarding scholarships or other awards. The range of awards available is intended to serve a variety of objectives, including educational, foreign policy, aid and trade. The question of the appropriate balance between these different objectives is another issue that has become explicit, rather than implicit.

The policy of full-cost fees has made everyone in higher education more aware of the importance of the overseas student market. The fact that the language of business: 'entrepreneurial activity', 'marketing', 'customer care', 'after-sales service' and 'value for money' is now often applied to questions of overseas student policy and recruitment is deplored by some, but can be seen as a reflection of an increased awareness that higher education is an investment for its students. Full-cost fees mean that the costs of that investment are explicit. The growing numbers of overseas students demonstrate that British higher education is regarded as a sound investment, by many, and the concern with 'responsible recruitment' and 'after sales care' shows an awareness that long run marketing strategies are more advantageous than short run income maximization. This gives grounds for some optimism as universities, colleges and polytechnics operate in the social market for British students and for research that the Government is organizing for them in the 1990s.

7

Effects of Funding Changes in Continuing Education*

Introduction

The number of students in universities taking part in continuing education courses in 1987/88 was 555,000. This was over 200,000 more than the total of full-time and part-time students on regular courses. Naturally the amount of time they spent in the university was much less, amounting on average to 25 hours per student. Nevertheless it is significant that in any year more people see the inside of a university for continuing education than as regular students.

This chapter examines the effects of developments in Continuing Education (CE) and the extent to which they were stimulated and shaped by changes in funding mechanisms. In particular, the programme of Professional, Industrial and Commercial Updating Programme (PICKUP) and the changed basis for the funding of In-Service Education of Teachers (INSET) are examined as examples of resource-led interventions within the broader strategy of encouraging higher education to look to industry, commerce and other clients for a larger share of its income.

CE includes a great variety of activities; it is widely dispersed through departments, faculties, and specialist centres and it is provided by an assortment of permanent, temporary, full time, part time, sessional, peripatetic, seconded, free lancing, moonlighting persons working in widely spread settings, sometimes collaboratively and often at times of the day, week and year when facilities, including staff, are not used for regular teaching. Suggestions for using university plant more intensively on regular courses should certainly take into account their effect on the availability of resources for CE. In spite of, or perhaps because of it, nearly all the case study institutions have made substantial efforts to regularize continuing education provision, by establishing centralized units, by improving information gathering and liaison functions, and by instituting uniform procedures for costing, pricing, and the allocation of income earned.

* A first draft of this chapter was written by Janet Harland

Some institutions have a lively tradition of community and adult education; these include the universities which had 'responsible body' status, and also others on both sides of the binary line which had a long history of providing for the local economy and community. In universities, particularly, there is some evidence of tension between traditional extra-mural, outreach work, and the more commercially driven priorities of recent short course provision. These opposing philosophies can cause tensions, especially where, as frequently happens, both functions are in the same administrative unit.

Administrative structures

Nineteen of the 24 case study institutions had strengthened their adminis-trative arrangements for CE between 1987 and 1989. PICKUP funds were an obvious stimulus to these developments but in more than half the institutions, expenditure on infrastructure had been greater than the specific grants for CE.

Twenty two of the 24 institutions visited had Units, Departments, Centres, or Offices (all subsequently referred to as 'units') to take charge of their CE development policies. In one of the others the Industrial Liaison Officer, on a salary paid partly from PICKUP funds, 'looks after' short course provision; in the other, there is a Dean of CE but only a loose structure to support him. The extent to which institutions have invested in their CE Units varies and there are widely different levels of support staff, premises, specific accommodation for short courses and other forms of facility for industrial and commercial clients. Nearly all the polytechnics were anticipating a substantially greater level of this kind of investment.

CE units are both outward-facing and inward-facing. As far as the outside world is concerned, they are concerned with marketing and promotion. Many represent their institutions on local and regional committees and collaborative panels with other higher education insti-tutions. They are the routine point of contact with the PICKUP Regional Advisers (though the importance attached to this link is often low). They are also usually responsible for bids for PICKUP funds.

Inward-facing functions include the dissemination of information to academic staff and with stimulating and regularizing departmental in-volvement in short course provision. Five institutions reported that their Units maintained, or were developing, databases on local industry. Encouragement is an important function though there is widespread comment that not all academic staff have the willingness, capacity or opportunity to participate. Sometimes there is no demand for what a particular department may offer; but often the staff feel themselves to be fully or more appropriately occupied with other teaching and research.

Fewer than a quarter of the CE units are themselves actively involved in the provision of short course programmes. Where they are it tends to be in the sphere of adult education, but also include Access courses and, in two instances, specific provision for small businesses. Much of the CE unit support takes the form of help in preparing budgets, establishing costs and fixing prices. Support merges into standardization and regularization. One of the main functions of CE units in nearly half the case study institutions is to bring separate departments into line with institutional policy. 'Pulling together a fragmented institution into a corporate whole is damned difficult', said one respondent.

Monitoring short course provision and keeping records are also key tasks. As institutions become more aware of how much existing work can legitimately be classified as CE, they are seeking to keep more comprehensive statistical information. Several interviewees believed that the total amount of CE was inevitably going to show a *statistical* increase for some time to come, because providers are realizing that some of the work that has been going on for years in a range of departments can, without distortion, be classified as CE.

Few of the CE units are seen as having a status equivalent to more traditional academic activities. As a consequence many of their staff see themselves as having a proselytizing function: they talk about changing attitudes and practices among colleagues, with a conviction that CE is of central importance to the future of higher education, and not only for financial reasons. It remains to be seen, however, whether it will ever become a mainstream activity of universities or polytechnics.

Another growing phenomenon is of short courses being provided by semi-independent centres, often within academic departments. As in the case of research and consultancy centres discussed in Chapter 5 the motivation has frequently been to provide a boundary between the institution's regular academic work and this quasi-independent activity, and to allow the operation of staffing and pricing policies that lie outside academic norms. In many cases consultancy centres and short course centres overlap. They are often prominent in the establishment of contacts with commercial and industrial sponsors. Where such centres are small-scale organizations wholly dependent on the departments that engendered them, they make little impact on the life of the institution: but where they generate sufficient income to develop an independent, corporate life of their own, with their own staff and their own constituency of support in the academic institution and in the surrounding community, then they can be an alternative to the traditional structures of university or polytechnic life.

Financial issues

Change and uncertainty surround costing and pricing of courses. There is general agreement that costs must be covered but not about what costs to include. Many courses have only a 'short shelf-life' but full development costs are rarely included. This raises questions about the long-term financial viability of some CE activities.

In only one of the case study institutions was specific reference made to targets for net contributions to central funds from short course revenue. A more common situation is for a short course programme to show a surplus in respect of the direct costs but to be insufficient to cover the costs of maintaining the necessary infrastructure. In one university finance office, it was claimed that the deficit would be reduced more by closing down the CE Unit than by trying to raise net revenue from short courses. Nevertheless senior managers in most universities and polytechnics are keen to increase their short course work. They provide departments with financial incentives through the arrangements for sharing fee income between central and departmental funds.

Overheads are much discussed but there is little common practice, or even insistence, in most institutions that rules or guidelines are consistently applied. Usually overheads are calculated on direct costs. Most universities name a figure of 40 per cent, with polytechnics usually quoting a lower figure of between 25 and 33 per cent. Many admit that they are not achieving these levels but believe that attempts to cover full costs would price many activities out of the market.

In addition to the general problems of pricing there is a wide range of activities which CE units believe should be included in their programmes but which cannot realistically be expected to generate cost covering fees. These include obvious areas of difficulty such as the unemployed, individuals who seek retraining in mid-career on their own behalf, access courses and the traditional forms of extra-mural adult education, but there are also frequent references to the public sector, including local authorities, as being unable or unwilling to meet an economic fee level. There are also industrial and commercial customers that are not profitable. One polytechnic department, with a flourishing programme of courses on the application of technology in design, reported that 'its' industry is organized in small units which find difficulty in meeting commercial fee levels: merely releasing staff is a major expense for them. Several other institutions highlighted the needs and difficulties of small, often new, businesses. However, references were also made to the reluctance of some larger concerns to pay rates which result in a useful surplus. One university quoted an offer of £300 from a public corporation for a course costed at £2000. A polytechnic referred to a contract it had with a major financial institution to provide training for its employees: the client was apparently only deterred from hiring freelance instructors at reduced prices by the realization that CNAA accreditation would be lost. The possibility of accreditation is an important constituent of the marketing strategy of many higher education institutions.

In a few places there was concern that staff can augment their income by 'moonlighting', sometimes undercutting their own institutions. However, head of CE Centres in several institutions also recognized that the opportunity for academics to earn additional funds from private consultancies is essential if higher education is to compete with the private sector for staff in subject areas where demand is high. This is why it is seen as important to develop incentives to encourage staff to seek opportunities for their own departments to provide short courses. Such incentives are not only in the form of direct payments: staff can feel rewarded by better facilities and equipment, and additional opportunities for research and development within their own departments.

Staffing

Sometimes short courses are staffed by academics from within the institution, but it is much more common for instructors to be recruited on a short-term, part-time basis. Such staff often have a tenuous relationship with the university or polytechnic. In several places difficulties were reported in recruiting suitable freelance staff and this was widely seen as a major constraint on the expansion of short course programmes. In one of the polytechnics it was said that the staffing difficulty is at its most acute in those specialisms where courses are in strongest demand from industry to remedy skill shortages, because these are the areas where potential tutors inside and outside the polytechnic have many alternative employment opportunities.

Use of the institution's own staff is obviously advantageous where it is possible. Clients often attend, or request, courses because they want the expertise and reputation of a particular department or individuals within it. Some departments have used the financial discretion available to devolved centres to employ CE staff on a semi-permanent basis. However, while for some the short course market is sufficiently predictable to offer favourable employment terms, many departments have to offer short contracts with all the problems of recruitment and retention discussed in Chapter 5.

The extent to which regular academic staff are rewarded financially for short course teaching varies between and within institutions, and is often determined by whether it is seen to be extra to normal work loads. There are significant differences between institutions in the recognition of short course work for promotion and appraisal. In many institutions no formal credit is given, while in others involvement in short courses is now seen as an important component of academic performance. In one institution, where serious attempts have been made to ensure that CE becomes a mainstream activity, it is now institutional policy to give full recognition to contributions in this field including promotion criteria and faculty performance indicators; the appraisal scheme reflects that policy.

Similar, though less explicit, policies were found in two other institutions, but in most there was no indication that academic recognition is given for short course work. This is undoubtedly one reason why CE

coordinators often experience problems in persuading academic colleagues to contribute to short courses. Conversely, it is equally likely that
the prevalent view of short course work as being of peripheral academic
value explains why it is not accepted as an important criterion of
performance. Most academic staff see a balance between research and
teaching on degree courses as their main source of professional reputation
and personal satisfaction. Instances were quoted of departments with large
potential markets for short courses (for example, in Computer Studies),
which nevertheless see their priorities elsewhere. A further explanation for
the low priority given to short course activity is that academic staff are
under all-round pressure and that this discourages them from seeking
what is seen as extra work. The establishment of systematic appraisal
strategies may give institutions an opportunity to modify their priorities.

Negative attitudes are, however, by no means universal and all the
universities, polytechnics and colleges visited had examples of successful
programmes; in a few, short courses were in the mainstream of their
academic programmes. Motivations vary among those who are actively
involved. Financial considerations are undoubtedly strong, but so too is the
public service ethic. Another factor is that many academics wish to stay in
touch with industrial and commercial fields that relate to their specialisms,
partly from a wish to build contacts and encourage other forms of
contracted work, but partly also from a genuine desire to update and
enrich their own knowledge.

Modes of delivery

Almost all the institutions visited provided evidence that the line between
award bearing and non-award courses is being blurred. Many are
developing short courses which can be taken as modules within a degree or
diploma course. They range from post-graduate courses in Science,
Engineering and Business Administration, to Certificate programmes
which allow the accumulation of adult education credits towards part-time
first degrees. An innovation in one university (and similar schemes exist in
several others) was that of intermittent one week intensive courses (30–40
contact hours), with 15 such modules required for the award of an MSc.
This kind of development can also grow from the opposite end because
many institutions are adapting modules from their degree programmes for
the short course market.

A small step from this is the recognition of modules completed at other
institutions and there are many examples of consortial arrangements to
facilitate such interchange. Polytechnics have made greater steps than
universities in this direction, with many taking advantage of the development of Credit Accumulation and Transfer schemes (CATs) which allow
for the accreditation of prior learning and experience in a variety of forms.
In one polytechnic all the students registering for degrees under this

scheme between 1986 and 1988 received some credit for prior experience, while 58 per cent obtained credit for more than half of the total requirements for the degree. Developments of this kind, coupled with participation in local PICKUP consortia and other forms of local and regional networks, are leading to some collaboration between institutions as, for example, in the Consortium for Advanced Continuing Education and Training in the Manchester area. However, relations between providers are also inevitably competitive and no evidence was discovered to suggest that there is likely to be significantly more co-operation in the near future.

Collaborative schemes with major clients are developing in many places. There are now many short course programmes devised in negotiation with particular companies and tailored to their specific needs, sometimes delivered in their premises and involving their personnel in the delivery of the course. Such courses are sometimes incorporated into award bearing programmes, with credit for prior learning arranged through CATs schemes. Some courses are run entirely by the companies concerned, with the higher education role confined to validation and accreditation.

The professional, industrial and commercial updating programme

The PICKUP Programme was established to meet the needs of employers in a rapidly changing work environment. It aims to help higher education institutions in their efforts to increase their provision for meeting such needs, by the development of infrastructures to support the work, and the encouragement of new teaching methods and approaches. It also aims to increase awareness among employers of the need for updating and of the way in which higher education can help them. As such, PICKUP addresses a large part of the general objectives of many higher education institutions in the provision of short courses, but not the whole: its focus is on collective and commercial, rather than individual needs.

The initial UGC and the NAB guidelines required institutions to set their bid for funds within a broader strategic plan for the development of CE and an estimate of how they intended to increase the number of courses offered, the number of students enrolled, and the amount of income from fees. Thus one implicit policy intention was to stimulate more development than that supported through the funds allocated. This encouraged institutions to reclassify existing courses under this heading.

There was some uncertainty about the purposes of PICKUP. The form in which bids had to be set gave the impression to institutions that they were to see short courses for employers as being largely concerned with the generation of fee income. This created a good deal of uncertainty, with many providers not being clear as to whether their overall CE programme should be seeking to recover direct costs or to make a net contribution to institutional funds. The wider the scope of the institution's aspirations in relation to CE (i.e., the larger its commitment to adult and community education as a whole), the more serious is the dilemma.

There is widespread concern about the rigours of the bidding process and the time it absorbs, in relation to the small scale of the funds available. It was claimed in one place that each bid involves up to 1 month's work. In another, the Registrar was sceptical as to whether the amount of money available through PICKUP had been enough to justify the trouble in getting it. However, in another institution it was acknowledged that formulating the bids had been a very good discipline and that PICKUP had achieved a big impact for a small investment. CE staff in several institutions commented favourably upon their relationship with the PICKUP Regional Advisers and on the benefits they had derived from the regional networks fostered by the advisory service.

In a few institutions the observation was made that the decision to bid for PICKUP funds had been prompted in part by a wish to maintain good relationships with the government and funding agency. This suggests that this kind of categorical funding can produce responses that are at least partly expressions of an anxiety to be seen as being cooperative. As such, there can be a distinct flavour of 'going through the motions'. Other comments suggest that many participants do not feel that their experiences of an externally funded initiative such as PICKUP feed easily into the mainstream development of the university or polytechnic.

The in-service education of teachers

The financial basis of INSET

This section examines INSET as a special instance of CE. Our enquiries concentrated not upon INSET in its broadest sense but specifically upon the impact of the Local Education Authority Training Grants Scheme (LEATGS) (which has since been transformed into Grants for Education Support and Training, GEST). Under this scheme, which was introduced in April 1987, INSET is funded under specific rather than general grants, payable to LEAs and schools after they have submitted an acceptable programme for each financial year, against an indicative allowance based upon teacher and pupil numbers.

This scheme contrasted with previous arrangements whereby LEA INSET costs were included within general grant. No coherent planning or policy was required from them, and significant aspects of the expenditure of any individual authority could be recovered under pooling arrangements. Higher education providers of INSET were able to recruit by direct appeal to individual teachers and to pursue policies which were not directly affected by the priorities of either local authorities or the DES. As a result the previous decade had seen a significant increase in advanced study for teachers, but also criticism that the courses offered were often somewhat remote from practical needs.

It is believed in most university and polytechnic education departments that the introduction of LEATGS on providers 'decimated' the numbers of full-time students on award bearing courses. There was also a reduction in the number of students following 'long short courses' (i.e. 20 days or more), especially in the PCFC institutions. A major factor is the unwillingness of LEAs, schools and colleges to allow protracted teacher release. In some institutions part-time numbers have compensated for these losses; this has been facilitated by modularization of courses.

One effect of the LEATGS was to narrow the gap between INSET and other forms of CE offered by higher education institutions. LEAs and locally managed schools now control funds which have previously been more directly available to higher education. They are thus in a real sense clients or customers. Higher education providers of INSET thus perform similar tasks to those already discussed for CE in general. It is not therefore surprising to find that many of the same problems, opportunities, and contradictory forces that characterize the wider provision of Continuing Education are operating in relation to INSET.

Administrative structures

Few institutions made substantial structural changes to accommodate LEATGS. However, several have given a senior member of staff specific responsibility for INSET developments; and in most case study institutions, individuals in a range of posts were identified with INSET initiatives. One major provider has reconstituted its University Centre for Teachers into an INSET Office. In a large polytechnic, short course provision for teachers has been concentrated in the School of Humanities and Education whose Dean now devotes much time to liaison and negotiation with LEAs. Elsewhere, however, the need to develop INSET is seen as part of the logic of dealing with diminishing enrolments on full-time award bearing courses and is thus a mainstream responsibility widely shared.

All institutions have revised their promotional activities. This is clearly no easy task ('we are amateurs at advertising'). Materials reaching one level of the system are not necessarily distributed to all who might be interested, and yet personal knowledge of a particular course is still a crucial factor in application and recruitment. In areas where alternative providers exist, the number and variety of courses on offer can be overwhelming, especially as anxiety about numbers has caused many providers to add to their existing programmes. Moreover many LEAs, through their INSET coordinators, are seeking to intervene between the providers, and the schools and teachers by setting out their own INSET menus in elaborate documents which include, but by no means particularly stress, higher education courses.

Many universities and polytechnics have developed semi-independent Centres with declared specialisms of the kind widespread in other CE activities. Some of these were established with support from the UGC or NAB funds earmarked for INSET; others originate from academic initiative money, or Training Agency grants, or charitable funds. Some were initially seen as vehicles for securing research funds. Such Centres are becoming an important focus for INSET, often benefiting from operating on the margins of institutional rules with respect to staffing and pricing.

A major task for higher education providers in the new context is to ensure a good relationship with their clients. There are regional networks which bring together LEAs and providers, but the development of genuinely co-operative regional structures is vitiated by the inherently competitive situation. So most institutions also aim to establish exclusive relationships between themselves and each LEA, and these run alongside the regional networks.

Despite all the formalized liaison much INSET results from close personal links with individual academics. Most academic staff in this field are in regular contact with practitioners in the LEA, its schools and colleges and the value of informal, personal contacts is widely recognized.

There is still much unease in the new relationships. Providers often view the LEA programmes as having gone for breadth rather than depth, and achieved little more than superficiality. (This remark echoes LEA comments that DES officials seem to be more interested in head counts than in either quality or coherent policy.) Higher education providers claim to find themselves 'selling' an INSET diet based on 'delivery skills' and 'knowing how', to the virtual exclusion of more open-ended and reflective approaches to professional development.

Many LEAs and schools, on the other hand, are still intoxicated by their independence and are attempting to sustain large do-it-yourself INSET programmes with little higher education input. Where 'experts' are required, they prefer to buy them in on an *ad hoc* basis and use them in school and teacher centre based courses, often using freelance or moonlighting lecturers as 'trainers'. One network is developing a database to produce a consumer-tested record of largely independent providers. Universities and polytechnics view these developments with some anxiety and they certainly affect the nature and quality of the relationships between higher education institutions and their clients.

Financial issues and costing

As in CE generally, there is serious concern about the financial viability of INSET short course and consultancy work. INSET providers are working within a severely constrained market: there are only a limited number of

LEAs to which each can offer its services, and some are very limited indeed for geographical reasons alone. Local authorities and schools are not free agents in that they are circumscribed by the conditions of grant and by the need to cope with the implementation of the 1988 Education Reform Act. Even among providers able to demonstrate notable speed in their transition to new ways of working, there is anxiety about the financial aspects of the operation. As one Director of INSET put it, they fear that 'there isn't enough money in the INSET system to keep it going'.

There are wide variations in costing and pricing. For example, in 1988/89 one polytechnic charged students between £26.80 and £48.30 for one evening a week across a whole year: another was charging £50 for a part-time one term module of an MA course, and this was due to rise by 50 per cent to come into line with overall institutional policy by 1991. One polytechnic charged £50 per day for Initial Training courses for teachers, while another in the same region charged only £30. In some places costing used back-of-the-envelope methods: for example, costing a short course in one polytechnic proceeds by 'calculating the teaching cost (£17 per hour at part time rate); doubling it; adding on charges for equipment, materials, rental of space, etc.; dividing by the number of recruits; and rounding upwards to give a fee level'. Such a strategy is certainly cost covering rather than profit maximizing. For example, it fails to capitalize on the well-subscribed courses in order to subsidize 'loss-leaders' which most institutions claim are essential.

The most difficult problem is costing development and preparation time. LEAs and schools want to spend their money in national priority areas and other topics of current concern. One respondent complained that the university 'has to keep developing expertise on an *ad hoc* basis according to the flavour of the year. As the initial development costs tend to be high, this represents a problem.' A polytechnic reported that income from 'full-cost GRIST courses [Grant Related In-Service Training – the predecessor of LEATGS] is not enough to cover preparation, planning, and so forth. But because the pattern of courses has to vary, it is often not possible to repeat courses, and thus recoup the development costs.' Another institution provided examples of preparation costs for a course in primary science: a meeting between three members of the college staff and LEA advisers had taken 12–16 hours of staff time; on their own estimate of £70 gross costs for an hour of a lecturer's time, the cost of this meeting to the college was around £1,000, and this included nothing for preparation and follow-up. There was no way in which the LEA would accept that this £1,000 constituted a legitimate part of the cost, and therefore the price, of this programme. If development costs are not recoverable within the price charged for INSET, it follows that they are being covered by hidden subsidy from other activities, and from access to resources such as expertise, buildings and facilities which have been developed and maintained under other budget headings.

One polytechnic with a strong tradition of short course work 'doesn't do a lot of INSET because the market doesn't pay very well'. The 'normal fee of £300–400 per week is not attainable'. This comment draws attention to the point made in virtually all the case study institutions that LEAs 'do not have a realistic policy on payment', 'are not used to paying full costs', and 'are having great difficulty in coming to terms with the new pattern of INSET: LEA culture makes it difficult for the college to extract full cost fees'. Some institutions are trying to deal with this situation by moving cautiously towards full-cost fees; others are 'trying to establish what the market will bear'. One large provider appears, at least temporarily, to have accepted the inevitable: in 1987/88 it calculated that the gross cost of a day's work by a member of the academic staff was £400 – it charged only £200, on the grounds that 'LEAs were unused to paying out such sums'.

Many institutions are reluctant to try for full costs, particularly when they are dealing with schools. One expressed this as the need to maintain the relationships that underpin access for teaching practice and research: 'goodwill relationships could change into financial relationships'. Another view was that 'one couldn't go the full cost route with teachers'. Several referred to the danger of provoking resistance in schools. Where the higher education institution is asking for favours *and* for money, schools may be tempted to ask why they may not charge for receiving a student on teaching practice. If the new relationship is not kept on a professional footing, there is a danger that schools might respond by declaring that they can manage INSET for themselves: 'now we can do our own thing in a glossy hotel!'. Higher education responds to such statements with self-interested alarm, but also with genuine professional misgivings.

Some Education departments have been seeking clients other than LEAs. Apart from contracts with off-shore islands (a somewhat limited market, contracts have been signed with health authorities, the police, banks, and the Training, Education and Enterprise Department (TEED) (formerly the Training Agency). At the same time, specialist departments other than Education have been taking advantage of INSET funds to offer updating courses to teachers.

As in the wider field of CE, the allocation of income from INSET earnings varies widely. At one extreme is the more or less autonomous cost centre. In one university, where the School of Education has been notably successful with INSET work, the School retains 90 per cent of the earnings which the university receives for the 100 FTE INSET allocation and also the whole of the £20,000 per annum CE money it earns. In return, the School accepts full responsibility for funding the 10 full-time equivalent staff employed on INSET work. But this is an extreme example. Other institutions expressed concern about the unpredictability of INSET earnings and the consequent difficulty of funding additional staff.

At the other extreme the experience of one university typifies the kinds of problem that arise in trying to develop an effective system of incentives in a centrally managed institution. The income from short courses and other forms of INSET goes to central funds, and departments are credited either with FTEs if they have not met the institution's target student : staff ratio, or with additional departmental allowances where they are above target. The problem with this system is that, in the absence of penalties for failing to meet student : staff ratio targets, there is little incentive to seek out opportunities for short course work or consultancies in those departments which have not reached their regular student number targets. The institution had recognized that both departments and individual staff needed positive encouragement, and discussions were under way to see how this could be achieved.

The issue of additional personal earnings for staff was raised in a number of places. As in Continuing Education generally, the case for overtime payments is much clearer cut in polytechnics where contact hours are defined and over-time rates known. None of the universities visited had a clear policy on this issue.

Modes of INSET delivery

One indicator of the 'mainstreaming' of much INSET work is that increasingly short course modules are being offered as modules within award bearing courses and teachers taking short courses are being encouraged to register for degree or diploma courses. Such registration qualifies for support from the higher education funding bodies, and thus allows the provider to charge a less than full cost fee. However, education-ists believe that the case for such integration is as much educational as financial.

Almost all the case study institutions indicated that there has been a move towards modularization. INSET shares with the rest of CE an increasing tendency to blur the edges between award and non-award bearing courses. The motivation is partly strategic and financial, (LEAs and teachers might be led by stages to commit themselves to award bearing courses); but it is also partly professional. Many academics believe that the shift to an INSET policy based primarily on immediate national and institutional needs has decreased opportunities for the personal and professional development of teachers, and that modularization of degree schemes with 'progression' built into them can compensate to some extent for this by encouraging individual teachers to construct programmes towards a recognized qualifi-cation that is appropriate to their interests.

Modules take different forms in different places. One key factor is geographical; in an urban area, a part-time module is typically taught on one evening a week, while in a dispersed rural area with campus accommodation the tuition may be concentrated into residential periods. Modules can be built up to achieve awards at various levels. At the lowest level, there are examples of Diplomas or Certificates in Professional Studies which are little more than the institution's mark of the satisfactory

completion of a specified total of modules. Above this, there are arrangements to continue the accumulation of credit towards B.Ed, B.Phil and a
range of Master's degrees, often requiring higher level modules plus
dissertations or projects based upon action research in the candidate's own
school or college. One polytechnic, which has committed itself heavily in
this direction, refers to 'pathways' through the modular programmes
which lead to a range of qualifications with a range of specialist biases. Some
of the institutions visited indicated that they had long been committed to
modular programmes but for many this is a new development, and some
are still not fully converted.

Two other issues are intimately bound into the moves towards
modularization: the first concerns the accreditation of school- or
LEA-based INSET towards a modular degree, diploma or certificate; and
the second arises from moves towards credit transfer between higher
education institutions. Within a wider trend towards the recognition of
work-based learning, higher education providers have recognized that
much useful INSET is now being provided within LEAs, or results
directly from development work within school or college. Moreover,
teachers are more likely to register for modular courses if they realize that
they can gain credit for work and experience undertaken as part of their
normal work.

Many institutions are therefore moving in this direction. Figures for the
total credit which can be acquired in this way varies between 12 per cent and
50 per cent. However, most providers wish to be involved in the off-site
experience from the outset, rather than merely to recognize a *fait accompli*
over which they have exercised no quality control. They are therefore
negotiating means of validating the school-based work through the
designation of 'support tutors' or 'named counsellors', thereby acquiring a
stake in the LEA's INSET programme. Our survey provided one interesting example where the provider has set out very clear guidelines for
teachers seeking this form of accreditation: the school concerned *must*
include the module fee within their INSET budget allocation; the teacher
concerned *must* be prepared to share the work with colleagues; and the
school's own INSET co-ordinator *must* have participated in the provider's
training programme (developed in co-operation with the LEA) concerned
with the management of staff development in schools. The provider
charges £100–150 for supporting the teacher through the module. A
variant of this arrangement was found in one university where the second
year of the MA degree is entirely school based, with the student's work
supported by supervisions on site, a scheme that is said to be very popular
with both the LEA and the teachers concerned.

The credit transfer initiatives taken by the Council for National
Academic Awards (CNAA) and the Universities Council for the Education
of Teachers (UCET) are arousing considerable interest. In general
universities thought they stood to gain from these developments. But at
least two of the polytechnics expressed some reservations: one reported

that negotiations about transfer between institutions had not so far been going well, because the intending collaborators were also competitors; and a second said that they are not keen because they fear that students may avoid polytechnics in the later stages of their courses in order to get a university qualification. But despite these reservations, it seems that once accreditation for school-based work is available, it will be very hard to argue against similar recognition for other courses. Frequently this is likely to operate within a defined consortium of providers.

In this changing scene, it is not surprising to find a range of disparate initiatives as higher education endeavours to find viable new modes of INSET provision. One university has developed a range of intensive one-term full-time courses which the LEA helps to devise and to teach. The teachers can add two terms' part-time study plus a dissertation to qualify for a B.Phil (Ed). Another LEA seconded one teacher from each of its secondary schools half-time over a year to work on their schools' Technical Vocational Education Initiative (TVEI) extension proposal with staff in three higher education institutions; their development work was then incorporated into a study programme leading to a recognized qualification. Several institutions report the development of teacher fellowship pro-grammes, whereby teachers on secondment work on an LEA agreed project under the supervision of a tutor. One university reported that all its MA work is now done on an outreach basis in teachers' centres around the county. Recruitment improves where the course goes to the teacher rather than the teacher to the course.

Part of the rationale for modularization is that the various modules will also be available as self-contained short courses. Over and above that, most institutions are offering a programme of short courses of their own devising, based on previous successes or informed guesses about likely demand in a changing educational environment. These were sometimes described as 'fliers' or 'promotions'. Some short courses are developed in conjunction with LEAs; where successful and likely to persist, they are rapidly incorporated into the modular menu. Some concern was expressed that where such courses are 'one-offs', they may be seen as 'responsive to needs' but in the absence of a proper system of evaluation the quality may decline.

Institutions invariably describe themselves as willing to negotiate and to respond to expressed needs. They are prepared to teach off-campus. One is offering 'Baker day' packages to schools. But such flexibility is not easy, especially in view of the development costs and the instant expertise needed to respond to a rapidly changing and wide variety of issues. A respondent in one university, which had previously prided itself on its capacity to provide 'custom-built courses', said that it was difficult to offer such a service to individual institutions; now that the LEA has devolved moneys to the schools, for all but the national priority areas, the customer is no longer the local adviser who was able to negotiate on behalf of a much larger clientele than the individual school.

Policy and attitudes to INSET

There was wide acceptance of the need to make INSET responsive to the working concerns of teachers. While not wanting to lose the traditions of scholarship and research which have grown up within the field of educational studies, nor to debar teachers from the chance to engage critically with broad educational issues, nearly all members of education departments in universities, polytechnics and colleges agree that INSET must stay close to the practice of teaching.

Although the major policy objective behind LEATGS was the reorientation of INSET, higher education providers have had to accommodate not only to changes in the work itself but also to a major shift in the basis of funding for a very significant proportion of their activity. Thus a concern for their financial viability, bringing with it notions of markets, clients, costs, prices, value for money and profitability, is an integral part of modern course development. There are thus two dimensions of change in which attitudes are having to adjust, the professional and the financial: providers of INSET have two kinds of 'perestroika' to manage simultaneously.

Positive attitudes and new policies are permeated with anxiety about how to survive financially. In the Education department of one polytechnic which has always enjoyed a particularly close working relationship with a large authority, this view was clearly expressed: 'This notion of the business world didn't previously cross our minds: the driving force was always system needs. But now we are accountable to the poly for balancing our budget and even making a profit'.

Where institutions have felt concern about the capacity of their local authorities and schools to handle their new budgetary powers efficiently, anxiety was sharpest. One lecturer said that 'it might have been more effective to allocate some funds to institutions rather than give the whole lot to the authorities'. Another interviewee said of the local LEA (which had retained national priority area money and devolved all the rest to schools, refusing to move beyond what it sees as the rigid framework imposed by the DES), that 'the LEA has been frightened into rigidity rather than analysis and lateral thinking'.

Policy implementation via resource management has both positive and negative effects; the response of higher education providers is varied, and stretches from the positive, the optimistic and the expansionist to the gloomy and apprehensive. However, the new funding arrangements are still of comparatively recent date. A major concern of most members of Education departments is how to survive until a new equilibrium is achieved. Most of them fervently desire a few years calm to consolidate their responses to any funding system.

8

Government Initiatives to Stimulate External Funding*

Introduction

This chapter examines four government initiatives which were intended both to promote national priorities and to stimulate higher education institutions to seek matching funding from other sources. They are the Alvey Programme on Information Technology (IT), the Engineering and Technology Programme (ETP), the Enterprise in Higher Education Initiative (EHE), and the Interdisciplinary Research Centres (IRCs). There is no attempt to evaluate the programmes in terms of their own objectives. These exist in other places (for example Guy *et al.*, 1991, Flemming, 1989). Rather the chapter examines the way in which the funding mechanisms in the four initiatives have influenced the organization and academic activity of academic institutions. In addition an effort is made to estimate the opportunity costs of bidding for funds in each case.

The Alvey Programme was launched in 1983 following the report of the Alvey Committee which had been set up to advise on the scope for collaborative research in IT in the light of increasing overseas competition. Its aims were to increase the competitiveness of UK IT suppliers; to assure a measure of self-reliance in important areas of technology; to strengthen research and development by rationalizing fragmented resources, particularly by encouraging higher education–industry collaboration; and to achieve specific technical targets in key enabling technology areas. The Department of Trade and Industry allocated £200 million for the programme in the expectation that another £150 million would be provided by the private sector.

The Alvey Programme brought universities, polytechnics, Research Councils, government departments and industry together in a way that would serve as a 'model which may usefully be extended and applied in other areas of research' (ABRC, 1987). The work was carried out by consortia of firms, academic teams and research establishments, a typical

* This chapter is based on draft reports prepared by Cari Loder, John Mace and Suzanne Silverman

consortium including two or three firms and one or two universities. 'Clubs' were set up to bring participants together and to act as an information exchanges. There were a few projects of a long-range or speculative nature in which close industrial involvement would have been difficult but these had industrial members, to advise on commercial aspects and timing for full industrial participation. At the peak of the programme in June 1987 115 firms were taking part with 56 universities, 12 polytechnics and 24 other research establishments. Eighteen academic institutions received over £1 million each. On average, each project had 3.9 partners, comprising two industrial and 1.9 academic partners per project.

Although partnerships between higher education and industry were well established before the start of the programme, Alvey produced a substantial increase in collaboration. In general, academic researchers who participated in the programme considered industrial involvement to have been beneficial to their own research interests and an effective mechanism for technology transfer. Some problems were perceived by the academics as a result of shortages of technically qualified staff and administrative delays in project start-ups and, in particular, the agreement of collaborative contracts. Many academics claim that the scale of government support was insufficient to enable the UK to catch up overseas competition. There was some discontent with the club structure as being unnecessarily time consuming in relation to the benefits it brought.

The ETP, known originally as the 'Shift' and later the 'Switch' to science and technology, was designed to increase the number of student places in areas of science, engineering and technology to which the Government attached particular importance at a time when higher education funding generally was being severely cut back. It was launched in 1985 and consisted essentially of about £45 million of earmarked UGC and NAB funds. In 1988/89, the UGC's share was £11.3m while NAB allocated £1.9m.

The first announcement of the programme was made in a UGC letter to universities in November 1984. It outlined a possible initiative and specified four principles that would govern it:

(a) the Government would indicate a target number of places and the disciplinary areas in which they should be provided;
(b) that extra resources would be strictly related to the costs of providing places for students not included in the universities' present admission plans;
(c) that the places would be allocated selectively, with the object of focusing expansion on departments of high quality which are best able to demonstrate that industry values their graduates and is actively willing to help teach them;
(d) that the Committee would be concerned to make cost effective use of the resources, and would allocate them in the light of costed proposals from universities.

Over 30 universities responded to the request for statements of interest, covering more than 250 Engineering Departments.

In March 1985, the Secretary of State announced a £43m ETP programme over a 3-year period. Phase I would cost £14.7m and provided for additional annual intakes of 475 undergraduate and 104 postgraduate students and Phase II would cost £28.3m and provided for additional annual intakes of about 1,000 undergraduates and 120 postgraduates. The two phases together were expected to make available over 3,900 new places in universities by 1990. In effect the UGC was acting as an agent for the DES, since the DES took the decisions about the overall number of places, the funds which would be allocated, the kind of courses to be funded and the criteria on which they were to be judged. The UGC simply administered the scheme.

A condition of inclusion in the programme was that participants should be able to demonstrate that they could attract significant contributions from industry towards the costs of courses for the extra students. In the event there was no verification of industry's contributions, the main monitoring by the UGC was of student recruitment. Four had money clawed back because their recruitment was too low.

In June 1985 the Government responded to protests from NAB about the failure to include polytechnics and colleges in the 'Switch' initiative, as it was by then known, and a similar though smaller programme was announced for the public sector, starting with the 1986/87 academic year. In a report by the NAB Secretariat, the importance of industrial support was stressed and the form of this support was specified. It included:

(a) financial assistance with equipment;
(b) financial assistance with accommodation;
(c) financial assistance with teaching staff (i.e. salary enhancements or commitments to consultancies);
(d) additional sponsorship of students on courses;
(e) loan of high-quality staff for part-time teaching purposes (including visiting professorships);
(f) 'teaching company' arrangements (involving joint work on research or development between industrial firms and academic institutions);
(g) provision of additional training places (e.g. for sandwich courses);
(h) commissioning of research work.

Polytechnics and major colleges with degree courses in engineering were invited to submit proposals. All 29 English polytechnics and the Polytechnic of Wales submitted proposals, together with one English and one Welsh college.

Five polytechnic proposals were identified as having the strongest educational merit, but NAB staff thought that in most cases a reduction in costs was required to meet the test of cost effectiveness. They were asked to reconsider their cost estimates. Another three polytechnics were recognized as providing good and relevant proposals for some courses, but they did not match the comprehensive strength of the first five institutions. NAB staff proposed that specific proposals from these three institutions should constitute a reserve list.

At its meeting in July 1985, the NAB Board pointed out the lack of regional balance in the successful proposals, since four of the first group of five institutions were in the Greater London area and all five were in the south of the country. The Board also felt that the subject balance was unfavourable to the advanced manufacturing technology area. Inclusion of the three reserve polytechnics would go some way to meet these objections. In October 1985, the Government announced that all eight institutions would be included in the programme.

EHE was launched in 1987 by the Secretary of State for Employment, with the support of the Secretaries of State for Education and Science, Trade and Industry, Scotland and Wales. The Initiative is run by the Training, Enterprise and Education Department of the Department of Employment, (formerly the Training Agency, and before that the Manpower Services Commission). The aim of the initiative is to 'encourage the development of qualities of enterprise amongst those seeking higher education qualifications'. In its first 4 years the programme has committed about £50 million for expenditure over 8 years.

EHE is intended to encourage higher education institutions to embed enterprise promoting activities within their core undergraduate courses. The main objectives were set out in the first *Guidance for Applicants*:

(a) Every person seeking a higher education qualification should be able to develop competence and aptitudes relevant to enterprise.
(b) These competencies and aptitudes should be acquired at least in part through project-based work, designed to be undertaken in a real economic setting, and they should be jointly assessed by employers and the higher education institutions.

(Training Agency, 1989)

Students who have attended a course in a higher education institution which is taking part in EHE are expected to:

(a) be more enterprising;
(b) have developed personal transferable skills;
(c) be realistically informed about employment opportunities, aims and challenges and make better career choices;
(d) be better prepared to take responsibility in their professional and working lives.

The benefits to employers are expected to include greater contact with higher education, a better appreciation of what it can offer them and a better understanding of what students and graduates can do. Participating employers also have the opportunity to assist universities, polytechnics and colleges in producing graduates with aptitudes and attitudes that are thought to be relevant and useful in industrial and commercial employment, and in other aspects of adult life.

It is an explicit intention of the TEED that EHE programmes should offer 'more than simple, bolt-on modules in Business Studies' and rather than displacing broad academic education by narrow vocational modules the new programmes are expected to be integrated with existing academic provision. One key way of achieving this is through staff development programmes that show how to encourage more active, participatory and 'enterprising' approaches to learning by undergraduate students. From the outset academic staff development was seen as a critical feature of EHE and institutions were expected to design appropriate staff training programmes. It was also expected that projects, secondments and staff and student exchanges with employers would play an important part. Over the first 2 years of an institution's contract it must attract support from industry and business, whether in direct funding or through provision of facilities and equipment, equivalent to around 25 per cent of the TEED funding. This should increase in later years of the programme.

At the end of 1988 all higher education institutions were invited to bid for sums of up to £1m spread over 5 years to carry out course and staff development activities which would bring about changes of the type outlined above. Those that were not ready to put in a full-scale bid immediately were invited to bid for a smaller amount of development funds during the first year of the programme to enable them to submit a full bid in the second year.

One hundred and twenty eight first-round bids were submitted of which 82 were for full funding. These initial bids were short statements registering an interest in preparing a submission. Following an initial selection from the outline proposals, twenty institutions were invited to prepare detailed proposals. The two-stage selection process was designed so that the majority of universities, polytechnics and colleges did not have to commit too much time and expense in preparing a full submission in the context of a process which was inevitably going to be selective and in the first year at least was going to require a certain amount of learning on the job by both bidders and evaluators of bids. Eleven institutions were selected for full funding during the first year of the Initiative. By 1991 EHE was being implemented in about 50 institutions.

In a preliminary report on this first phase published in January 1989 the Training Agency announced that the criteria on which the submissions had been judged were:

(a) evidence of a substantial commitment to enterprise education;
(b) a broad understanding of what enterprise in higher education would mean and what it would do for students' learning styles and staff development;
(c) the commitment of the whole institution and the commitment of a significant number and range of employers to participate in the programme;

(d) that an assessment of the present curriculum had been carried out to identify where enterprise learning existed or could realistically be developed;

(e) evidence that an assessment of existing employer involvement in course design, delivery and assessment had been carried out;

(f) a commitment to sustain the programme beyond the period of pump-priming support;

(g) a plan for curriculum development and for integrating EHE into the curriculum by departments or course teams;

(h) a plan for successful staff development phased over five years; (projects/secondments/exchanges with employers might play an important part in that plan);

(i) a plan for employer partnership and involvement in the design, implementation and resourcing of the programme with predictions and costing of employer input;

(j) a plan for the management and co-ordination of EHE and its integration with existing management structures;

(k) a plan for monitoring and evaluating the progress and success of EHE and for feeding-back the results into the Initiative's continued improvement.

A common set of performance indicators agreed between the TEED and the institutions taking part in EHE includes: the amount of EHE activity, numbers and proportion of students involved, the types of assessment used, student outcomes, the amount of employer participation, the amount of staff development activity, and the type of staff developer.

Proposals for IRCs were presented to the Government in May 1987 in the ABRC's document *A Strategy for the Science Base* (ABRC, 1987) which concluded that there was a need for greater concentration and more strategic planning of university research (ABRC, 1987, p. 6). The Strategy document is translated into advice to the Secretary of State for Education in the Report *Science and Public Expenditure, 1988* (ABRC, 1988). IRCs began to be established by the Science and Engineering Research Council and the Economic and Social Research Council from 1988 onwards with the aim of concentrating research efforts, encouraging interdisciplinary work, increasing effort in important areas of strategic science, stimulating a readier and stronger interface between strategic research in higher education and industry and ensuring more positive and purposeful management of research within higher education. By 1990 about £120 million had been committed over a 5–10 year period.

In March 1988 the first IRC was established at Cambridge University. It had a guaranteed income from the Science and Engineering Research Council (SERC) of £5.3m over a 6-year period for research into superconductivity. By the middle of 1989 a further 16 IRCs had either been established or were in the process of being established.

An interim review of the IRCs was published in 1989 (Flemming, 1989).

Its main recommendation concerns the future development of IRCs. Whilst recognizing that the IRC initiative 'catalysed, and gave urgency, to discussions about new interdisciplinary structures' (Flemming, 1989, p. 27) the Report, after examining the process of bidding and selection, comes to the conclusion that:

> in future IRCs should be developed in a rather different way. This view is based on our belief that the IRC mode of funding should be considered as one of a number of possible ways of funding; and that a decision to follow the IRC mode in a particular case should emerge from the normal processes of reviewing areas, and deciding priorities, rather than through a special exercise.
>
> (Flemming, 1989, p. 28)

The Committee recommended that bidding should in future be limited to those Higher Education Institutions with the strengths to put forward first rate proposals. No further bid, they also conclude, should be made by the ABRC for 'an additional sum of money specifically to fund a further earmarked programme of IRCs. Resource needs should be judged in the normal way against competing claims'.

The Flemming Report is critical of the management structures of several of the IRCs and expresses concern about the possibility of what it describes as the 'asset-stripping' of departments. It says that the relationship between IRCs, subject cost centres and the research selectivity exercise needs to be clarified to allay departmental fears about losing their high rating and the recognition and departmental allocations associated with high research rating. The report is also doubtful about multi-site research centres. The argument for this approach was that it enabled expertise in more than one university to be combined in a single research enterprise, rather than being in a position to attract the best researchers from other places. It allowed smaller institutions to have some share of the IRC cake. The Report, however, argues that the vision of 'the IRC initiative was to concentrate effort, and one might reasonably suppose this to imply that the team would at least be gathered together in one institution' (Flemming, 1989, p. 34). Flemming concludes that a multi-institutional IRC is 'stretching an already stretched concept to the limit, and (has) doubts about how effective it can be.'

A common characteristic of all the four programmes outlined above is that institutions were required to bid for funds on a competitive basis in accordance with specifications set out by the funding agency, and the bids were assessed by the funding agency. Of the four programmes ETP and EHE were concerned with teaching; Alvey and IRCs with research. Only ETP was funded through the main higher education funding agencies, and this was on the basis of specific government funding for this purpose. The programmes operated at different times, and public funds were intended to help lever funds from the private sector so it is difficult to make a realistic estimate of their place in the total of higher education funding but annual public spending on all the programmes together never amounted to more than £90 million (Alvey £40mn, IRC £20mn, ETP £15mn, EHE £12mn). This was less than 3 per cent of the total recurrent income of higher education institutions.

The bidding process

In general, few serious problems were reported in bidding for Alvey projects, since, as one university professor stated, 'we all knew the ground rules'. While in one university only 2 out of 10 bids were successful, most participants thought that the success rate was sufficiently high to warrant the time and effort involved in preparing bids. The Alvey programme was contrasted favourably with other initiatives, such as the IRCs, which involved less chance of success and more uncertainties. However, the need to coordinate the bidding process with collaborating companies and other educational institutions was thought to have complicated the development of proposals. In one university for example concern was expressed about the time required to draw up a proposal for a project involving three universities and three companies, but they knew from an early stage that the scheme was likely to be successful.

In some institutions it was claimed that the time available between the initial announcement of the programme and the deadline for submitting bids was too short. The need to respond quickly encouraged one large devolved university to move toward a 'more managerial decision-making style in order to get the interested people in various parts of the university together'.

Estimates of the time taken to prepare bids ranged between 1 and 9 months of staff time, with individuals involved often being at professorial level. One professor, who described the costs as 'not exorbitant', estimated about 20 man days for each collaborating institution. The need for several meetings between collaborators, involving additional travel and subsistence costs, made estimates difficult. One university estimated the opportunity cost to be £10,000 over a 6-month period for a grant of £1.4m, a benefit–cost ratio of 140:1 for that project, but this would fall to 28:1 if all institutions had as little success as the university described in an earlier paragraph.

In the case of ETP the main factor in academic staff assessment of their experiences of bidding was whether they were proposing to mount new courses or whether they were merely adding extra students to existing courses. At one university, which increased student numbers on existing courses, the preparation of the bid was estimated at 6 weeks of academic staff time plus some support staff time; at another university, time spent by senior staff on internal discussions and discussion with other staff, government agencies and industry was estimated as equivalent to 20–25 man days.

In general the amount of time spent preparing bids is difficult to evaluate, since it included different kinds of activities. Some estimates include liaison work with industry to generate support, meetings with government agencies and other time spent in discussions, while others include only internal preparation time. For example, at a University where major building work was involved, the professor estimated that he spent 50 per cent of a year of his time preparing the bid, planning the building, liaising with architects, and so on. Another university also found the bidding difficult because it involved capital funding, but the Bursar estimated it took one man month to co-ordinate the bids, with one man week from each of the two departments involved (on two successful bids), but he restricted his estimate to the actual preparation of the bid for the UGC. Where figures are available the opportunity cost of bids in terms of the staff time involved seems to have averaged rather less than £5,000. With 30 university bids and an average annual disbursement per university of about £260,000 the 'benefit-cost' for the first year of the programme would be about 52:1 and this would be better if account is taken of subsequent years of the programme where by common agreement the opportunity cost of bidding was much less. The main reason for this favourable figure is that few of the bids were 'wasted', in that most of the universities that applied received something. It is probably the case also that where the probability of success is high the bidding is seen as less competitive so less effort needs to be put into preparing a proposal.

It was not possible to obtain sufficient information from the polytechnics to make any similar estimates but the efficiency indicator may be somewhat worse in that there were thirty initial bids and only eight awards made. If in other respects the costs and benefits were similar to universities the 'benefit-cost' figure would be about 14:1.

All the institutions involved in preparing new courses found the original bid the most time consuming to prepare, since subsequent bids were based on a carry-forward of the original bid based on actual recruitment. At a university where two new courses were developed, the professor estimated that the bid took several weeks of his time and substantial time from the departmental administrator, plus time devoted to committees and central administration. He felt that the short time scale was a real problem, failing to take account of the long planning period required to mount new courses, recruit staff, agree on the curriculum and recruit qualified students.

At another university the view was expressed that one of the most positive aspects of ETP was that there was a good probability of obtaining a significant amount of money at the end of the bidding process. Other initiatives, it was claimed, involved as much effort with either a low probability of success or little monetary reward for those that were successful. ETP was felt to have a high success rate for bidders compared with other competitive initiatives.

The Dean of Engineering at a polytechnic felt that ETP gave them an incentive to act quickly to mount a new course which they wanted to do anyway. While the bid was difficult to prepare because their records were not in good shape to support it, 'the need to demonstrate our strengths and express things concisely was not a bad thing in itself'. He felt many heads of departments had to spend a lot more time compiling information, but they need to learn to be better managers and have efficient information systems.

Some university respondents complained that the UGC did not provide enough guidance. At one it was claimed that it was a form of 'blind bidding' since they did not have information on how other bidders would behave or detailed guidelines on how to prepare the bids. At another there were complaints that they lost out for purely political reasons – it was claimed that the university was taken off the list in favour of Welsh and Scottish bids and it only succeeded at the last minute because some institutions were unable to spend their money.

Problems were reported in one university because the bidding guidelines did not take account of inflation in either the grants for equipment or recurrent expenditure. 'When the programme extended over 4 years this was a serious problem.' In a period when equipment costs were rising rapidly, it meant they could not buy all the necessary equipment from the grant and replacement and maintenance costs were also going up. It was claimed also that the terms of the bid also did not allow for the 23 per cent increase in staff salaries awarded after the grant was allocated.

Amongst the case study institutions only four, all universities, did not make a bid for EHE funding in the first year. Of these only one, a monotechnic post-graduate institution, did not intend to put in a bid in the second year. A major factor was the desire not to appear 'anti-enterprise'. A large research orientated university reported that its unsuccessful bid did not generate much enthusiasm within the university. The bid was made because the university 'did not want to appear anti-enterprise'. Another university claimed that it did not bid in the first round because the limited local industrial base made it 'difficult to assemble quickly a consortium of employers, which seemed to be a Training Agency prerequisite.' However, it was now believed in the university that 'it is impossible to ignore the political implications. If an institution does not participate it runs the risk of being seen as anti-enterprise and could suffer in many ways as a consequence . . . the college has no option but to show willing'. Another institution which in the first year 'did not bother to apply' reported that 'since then there has been a transformation of attitudes' and subsequent proposals were 'wholeheartedly supported'. It was thought that the Initiative would attract students and help to generate income from industry.

Four of the bids of case study institutions, two universities and two polytechnics, were successful. Among those that made unsuccessful bids in the first round, five (three universities, one polytechnic and one other institution) thought it unlikely that they would be submitting a bid in 1989. Their decisions were strongly influenced by a number of problems which they identified with the bidding process. Although most of the remaining

Table 8.1   Estimated cost of bidding for the Enterprise in
Higher Education Initiative 1988

	Universities *(£)*	*Polytechnics* *(£)*
Successful bids	16,000	11,000
Unsuccessful full bids	15,000	9,500
Outline development bids	2,500	1,500

15 still planned to make bids, several had decided not to invest too much
time and effort in the process.

Twelve of the 20 case study institutions which submitted bids to the
Training Agency were able to give reasonably clear estimates of the resources used in making the bids. These include an assessment of the value
of staff time and any other direct costs to the institution but exclude any
allowance for the value of the time of people from outside the institution
who may have been involved in the negotiations. For example one (successful) bid involved attendance at a seminar by representatives of 70 companies. Assuming this was a half-day seminar the opportunity cost of
attendance must have been at least £5,000. This has been ignored.

In some cases the institutions gave their own financial estimates and also
indicated the basis on which they were made. A few gave estimates of the
number of days of staff time involved. These were converted to cash at the
rate of £200 per working day for academic staff and £50 per day for
support staff. The results are the estimates shown in Tables 8.1 and 8.2.

There are two striking features about Table 8.1. The cost of bidding
claimed by the universities was considerably higher than for the non-
university institutions and successful bidders spent more on their bid than
the unsuccessful ones. The difference between universities and polytechnics may to some extent be due to differences in accounting practices.
All the universities in the case studies were conscious of the debate about
indirect costs and probably ensured that all such costs were included. The
public sector institutions however, until 1 April 1989, had little direct
experience of full-cost pricing and there may have been some tendency to
include only directly observable costs.

On the basis of these figures it is possible to arrive at an estimate of the
total real cost to the higher education system of the first round bids to the
Training Agency. From the evidence given by the Training Agency to
enquiries from the case study institutions it appears that there were 128
outline bids for full funding or for development funds and a shortlist of 20
were invited to develop a full proposal. Of these 20, 11 received support.
Table 8.2 shows the estimated total cost of the bidding process on this basis.

In broad terms Table 8.2 suggests that about £440,000 was spent in
bidding for projects which would bring in an income to the successful

Table 8.2   Estimated total cost of bidding for EHE funds in 1988

	Number of bids	Average opportunity cost per bid (£)	Total cost of bidding (£,000)
Outline and development bids only	108	1,833	198
Unsuccessful shortlisted bids	9	11,300	102
Successful bids	11	12,750	140
Total	128	3,440	440

Average opportunity cost per bid is a weighted average of the figures in Table 11.1 based on the following assumptions. Successful bids, 4 universities and 7 other institutions. Unsuccessful full bids, 3 universities and 6 other institutions. Outline and development bids, 36 universities and 88 other institutions. All figures have been rounded.

institutions over a 5-year period of about £10m – a benefit–cost ratio of about 23.

One concern frequently mentioned was an assessment of the chances of success. With the large number of applications and the relatively small number of successful bids, there was some doubt about whether it was worth the effort. The uncertainty was stronger in institutions that faced various kinds of handicaps, such as being in regions where the competition was very stiff and other institutions were seen to have the edge or, in the case of some institutions, being located in rural areas without an industrial hinterland.

Other problems mentioned involved various Training Agency require-ments, such as the need to involve the whole institution or aspects of the funding, and the failure to include overheads to cover full institutional costs. There was a feeling in one university that 'after mature reflection the problems with the administration of the Initiative outweigh the potential benefits of the additional funds and the possible curriculum developments that it permits.' None of the 40 or so respondents with whom the EHE was discussed expressed any hostility to the aims of the Enterprise Initiative but there was a strong feeling in some places that some of the Training Agency requirements were not reasonable.

In one university it was claimed that 'the requirement for the Initiative to cover the whole institution was not practicable'. The university had put in a 'compromise bid which caused great flak'. However, the process of compiling the bid had generated interest in some areas; engineering and education were mentioned specifically and they intended to develop 'enterprise components' within their own courses.

The one polytechnic that was unwilling to try again reported that it was difficult to co-ordinate an institute-wide bid and having spent over £3,000 on making the bid it was unhappy about the lack of constructive feedback from the Training Agency. It was felt that the central management of the institution was fully occupied with preparations for corporate status and had no time to be involved with peripheral activities which were unlikely to be successful.

In several institutions it was claimed that the bidding process was made more difficult by the tight timetable and the lack of specific information about the criteria on which the bids would be judged. One polytechnic respondent described the process as being like 'trying to get hold of jellyfish' and one university administrator felt that the goal posts had been moved when the second stage bids asked for considerably more financial detail than the Training Agency had originally indicated would be necessary.

In two universities which did not intend to make a bid in 1989 rather specific reasons for dissatisfaction were expressed. Both were universities that considered they had a public image of considerable employer involvement with their academic work and there was undoubtedly an element of pique in this not having been recognized by the Training Agency in its initial allocation. 'The question of whether the Initiative was designed to help get enterprise activity started in institutions which traditionally did not have much of this type of work, or whether it was simply to encourage this activity at all levels was not made clear by the Training Agency.' The Vice-Chancellor of one university which had 'put considerable time and effort' into its bid had learned 'that it was unsuccessful because the Agency considered it more appropriate to support institutions with a low level of existing activity.'

In the other disillusioned university we were told that their bid had had a strong commitment from the chairmen of all departments in the university. The bid had cost some 3 months of academic staff time to put together and was extremely detailed. However 'in the end the Training Agency seemed to pay no attention to the points indicated but appeared to make its decision based on a cursory examination of the front page.' Several respondents in this university expressed dissatisfaction with the way the selection had been conducted. Furthermore, close examination of the Training Agency financial regulations had 'shown that the Enterprise Initiative and other Training Agency activities resulted in a net loss for the university'. Doubts were also expressed about the management structures imposed by the Training Agency and the infringement of university autonomy.

In another university with substantial existing involvement with industry and, it was believed, a strong commitment to 'enterprise' in its undergraduate courses it was decided to bid for development funds in the first round because there was a wish to test the nature of the scheme before becoming too deeply involved. It was felt that 'the university ought to keep in touch with what was going on . . . it wanted to be in the information network'. However, as the process of bidding proceeded there was a growing feeling amongst senior staff in the university that it was 'an unseemly rush and it seemed that a lot institutions were more interested in getting their hands on the cash than in thinking what they might have to do if they received the cash . . . it was unreasonable to expect that higher education should suddenly drop everything to prepare bids for the Training Agency. It suggested that there was some slack in the system which was certainly not true of this university.'

Amongst the universities intending to put in further bids senior staff in one were very disappointed at their lack of initial success. However, they considered themselves to be members of an enterprising university and that 'it is therefore essential to show strong interest in the scheme'. Considerable effort was being put into writing and rewriting the second bid in the light of an assurance that 'all proposals of sufficiently high quality will be supported' and it was only because such an assurance was received that they agreed to spend so much time of so many staff in preparing the second proposal. This university was one of several where concern was expressed that the Training Agency does not provide funds to cover the costs of making a bid:

> 'In the world of consultancies it is common practice to include in any project the costs of making the bid to receive the contract. Often such figures are hidden in terms of overheads, but whatever label is given to them good accounting practice requires that the costs of making bids are budgeted for. Indeed the cost of successful bids has to carry the expenses incurred in unsuccessful bids, which is one reason why consultancy overheads are so high.' Nevertheless this university decided to make another bid in 1989 and estimated the combined costs of the two bids at about £15,000 mainly in terms of academic and support staff time in preparing them. 'The experience has helped to highlight the problem of how the cost of bids should be estimated and who should bear them.'

In the unsuccessful polytechnics less bitterness was expressed about their lack of success. One which was shortlisted to the last 20 did receive a development grant and 'will be disappointed if we do not succeed the second time around'. This polytechnic has substantial links with industry and it aimed to build its Initiative around these links. 'It was mainly a matter of co-ordinating what was already going on . . . there was no need to start any completely new activity to meet the Training Agency specifications.' In another polytechnic which was unsuccessful first time it is believed that its first bid had insufficient employers' support, and attempts are being made to overcome this for the second bid.

Of the 24 institutions studied 14 had bid for IRCs, either as prime or secondary contractors. Only two of the bids were from polytechnics. Six of the institutions, all universities, had been successful. There was widespread concern about the process of bidding for IRCs. It is a complex, lengthy and, we were informed in all 14 institutions that had put in bids, costly exercise. The problem was exacerbated by the short period allowed for the preparation of bids. One comment was 'the time scale was ridiculous – the whole physics community in the UK had from 1st July to 1st December to prepare their cases for the surface science bid'. The actual length and cost depends on the number of rounds that the institution remains in the bidding process, the degree of collaboration planned with other institutions and individuals, and the planned involvement with industry.

A common complaint was the problem of what many institutions referred to as the Research Councils 'moving the goal posts' or even 'moving the pitch'. One example was of advice being received from the Chairman of SERC in which collaboration was stressed being immediately followed by another letter in which 'the Chairman decided that collaboration should be minor, not part of the basic structure'. Another criticism of the process wider than that of 'continually moving the goal posts' is worth quoting in full:

> I would like to get a message across to the Research Council and to the ones that sit on top there, that it was not entirely a function of their behaviour, but these post contract negotiations have been infinitely complicated by continual changes of demands from the bureaucracy, in particular their habit of issuing one-week deadlines for extremely important decisions which involve tremendous amounts of time, and demanding that we work to these, but being themselves unable to answer even the simplest questions. We have said to them 'in 2 months time you will be asking us for this. Could you please clarify the guidelines so we can start preparing?' They say 'no, I'm sorry we can't, but we'll give you good notice when the time comes up'. Two months later they ring up and say they want such and such in a week. I think this is a message that must get through. Quite a lot of our costs are due to the fact that we are just not able to work in a reasonable fashion. We have to drop everything and it is not as if it is just one initiative in a very small department, there are three or four that have been active during this period.

Two other cases were widely quoted as examples of the moving of the goal posts. One case is where SERC had promised two awards, but made only one and the other is where bids were asked for and no award was made at all. It was claimed that no explanation was offered for these changes of policy and this illustrates another complaint about the process – the absence of feedback about the reasons for policy changes or why individual bids had failed.

The Flemming Report is critical of the bidding process. After commenting on the value that the initiative had in stimulating discussions about new interdisciplinary structures it states the disadvantages as:

(i) submissions were prepared hurriedly, and without as much detailed preparation as they really warranted;

(ii) institutions were having to give commitments which had not been fully thought through;

(iii) applications were being made without a clear understanding of what was expected, and expectations themselves changed during the process;

(iv) a great deal of nugatory work was done, notwithstanding the general advantages of undertaking the interdisciplinary discussions, as noted above.

Bidding for IRCs involves large opportunity costs in terms of time and also, in some cases, of cash directly. Making a bid is seen by most universities and some polytechnics as a signal to Research Councils that the institution sees itself as a centre of excellence in a particular field. They often believe that if the signal were not given they would lose out on other Research Council awards as well. This view is supported by the evidence of some institutions which came 'second' and claim that as a result they have subsequently been awarded programme grants. Thus for many institutions the costs of IRC bidding were believed to be unavoidable.

Few institutions had any precise record of resource costs of bidding but *every* institution said the manpower cost of bidding was very substantial. However, in a number of cases we were provided with the estimate of costs in staff time or money. These estimates are given in Table 8.3.

Table 8.3 Estimates of costs of bidding for IRCs in case-study institutions

Institution	Costs in non-monetary terms	Approximate money cost (£)
A	262 days	52,000
B	340 hours	10,200
	9 weeks	6,300
		16,500
C	35.75 man-days	7,000
D		50,000 to 100,000 (plus more if space included)
E	12 man-months + committee work + (professor's salary)	40,000
F	2,821 hours	85,000
G		100,000
H		250,000
J		10,000

A number of assumptions have been made in translating hours, days and weeks into a monetary figure. These are: 1 hour = £30; 1 day = £200; 1 week = £700. Where figures were given in monetary terms the basis for the figures was not given.

Although institutional costs vary enormously they are always substantial – the minimum is £7,000 for an unsuccessful bid in institution C. One of the most reliable estimates is that for institution F. This was a successful bid from a prime contractor; it is one of the larger institutions and it had documented more carefully than most the hours devoted by individuals, and committees. The figure was described nevertheless as 'a very rough estimate'. Another significant feature of this institution is that there was little time-consuming external collaboration in the bid.

Because of the variation in institutional cost estimates and the different number of bids for different IRCs in any estimate an average cost of bidding per IRC is inevitably a rough and ready guide. However, we can make crude estimates of the order of magnitude of the benefit–cost ratio. Each IRC seems to have attracted between ten and a hundred initial bids. If we take the lowest cost estimate of £7,000 and assume that 50 institutions put in initial bids of this price, we can estimate that institutional opportunity costs were of the order of £350,000. These costs are considerably higher than bids for the other initiatives considered. The main reason is the relatively high proportion of unsuccessful bids. If we take the relatively reliable estimates of Institution F and also assume five full second-round applications at this price, cost of this round would be of the order of £425,000. This would give a total bidding cost of just over £3/4m for a contract of around £10m a benefit–cost figure of about 13 which is considerably lower than the other initiatives examined in this chapter. It must be emphasized that the figure is very sensitive, depending on the number of initial bids and the size of the short list as well as the actual resources devoted to bidding in each institution. For example, if we had assumed 25 rather than 50 preliminary bids and three rather than five full bids we should have arrived at a benefit–cost ratio of around 23.

The figures given in this section are not easy to evaluate in the absence of a series showing similar estimates for other ways of allocating funds to higher education institutions. Another way of interpreting the benefit–cost figures given is that between 1 and 7 per cent of the resources made available in the various initiatives is used up in the process of bidding for them. However, there was widespread acceptance that although bidding is expensive, and although there is often some disruption of research and other academic work, the formulation of a bid in collaboration with others inside and outside the institution does encourage a clarification of aims and objectives and ways of achieving them that is often absent when funds are more easily come by.

There is a good case for agencies inviting competitive bids to monitor the costs of bidding and to adopt selection procedures that minimize them. Clear guidelines would help, as would early advice of the probability of success. It would also help institutions to receive prompt feedback on their bids and the reason for their failure. It should certainly be possible for at least the successful institutions to recoup the costs of bidding. Otherwise the costs of bidding are inevitably subsidized out of funds received from other sources.

Management and administrative issues

The fact that collaboration was one of the major aims of the Alvey programme meant that administrative costs tended to be high, especially in terms of staff time. While most institutions felt the programme was broadly successful many expressed reservations about the costs involved in establishing and managing consortia. In addition to the added costs of the many meetings between partners, which were seen as expensive in terms of both staff time and expenses, some institutions reported difficulties in getting everyone working together.

In the view of some respondents problems arose from the fact that companies do not have the same priorities as university researchers. For example, one collaborating company was mainly interested in selling hardware, while university staff were more concerned with software development. Another university reported that it was difficult to get the consortium to work, with so many different kinds of people trying to work together. The head of department felt that the pattern of work expected by the industrialists and the academics was very different. He had to paper over a lot of cracks where they were really doing uncoordinated work. One polytechnic participant found 'coping with the problems of collaboration was very time consuming'. Another institution had problems liaising with larger companies, mainly stemming from companies changing staff or losing interest in the project.

Along with the problem of differing priorities, there was a belief in some institutions that academic staff were at a disadvantage in dealing with industry because of the need to employ many university researchers on fixed term contracts. Contract researchers were sometimes not integrated into the general work of the department and felt patronized by permanent staff and they had no security of employment and were paid less than staff employed in private industry.

One university head of department said that 'any commercial company which threw out all its top specialists after 3 years and replaced them with new ones would go bankrupt, yet this is the way universities operate with research staff'. It was difficult for universities to offer long-term contracts when the Alvey funding was only for a fixed period, but he claims that in his department they have 'learned their lesson and written much higher salaries into bids for ESPRIT projects'.

A problem which was unique to the Alvey programme as far as the group of initiatives reported here is concerned was the negotiation of intellectual property rights. Most institutions reported some problems in this area, which is a potential source of conflict in any programme to increase collaborative research between industry and higher education. While the public funding bodies saw their investment in terms of 'pre-competitive' research, there were, nevertheless, bound to be difficulties in an area which had the potential to generate a great deal of profit.

A major concern for many academic staff was the delays in getting projects off the ground while an IPR agreement was negotiated. One university professor claimed that work which would have been done anyway, through SERC grants, was delayed under Alvey by IPR problems. Another felt that IPR relations were in general handled badly, particularly by their industrial partners. However, although this was obviously a point of concern for the institutions concerned, many research projects were able to begin before a collaboration agreement was signed.

Another source of criticism was cases where academic staff were personally involved in negotiating with industrial partners. One university professor felt that the scientists 'shouldn't have to waste time dealing with this issue, which should be left to the administrators.' Where the negotiations were handled by administrators delays over IPR were less of a problem, since projects were able to go ahead without finalizing the arrangements. One university did not actually sign the contract until the end of the 4-year project, while another waited 3 years. Where institutions were inexperienced in dealing with IPR, they may have had unrealistic expectations of the potential returns, but there were some suspicions that companies would seek to retain sole ownership of all the findings, although there does not seem to have been any serious attempts to prevent academics from publishing non-commercial findings in academic journals.

One professor thought that the problem of Intellectual Property Rights is not that of a company exploiting the university: rather it is that the company may prefer to keep such knowledge out of the public domain. This means there is no market mechanism to identify the value of the output, and its full financial significance may never by visible. As a result, 'it will be hard for the government to assess the value of the programme or the university to assess the royalties which should be paid.'

The management of the ETP raised different issues in that it largely involved additional resources to already existing departments. Its impact depended on the scale of the programme and the size of the departments in which it was located, whether courses were new and innovative, and their ability to generate industrial support. One widely appreciated aspect of the initiative was the equipment secured as a direct result of the programme, or as a spin-off from improved contacts with industry. The Dean of one polytechnic referred to the importance of up-to-date equipment when training students to work in industry and the difficulty of replacing obsolete equipment in high-technology areas, where it is constantly changing and budgets are very tight. A university professor considered the increased equipment grants to be extremely important and to have helped reorientate the department. In another university the capital input from industry was considered to have been extremely important for the establishment of a new Computer Science degree, but it was pointed out there is still a problem for the university in finding the money to cover recurrent running costs.

Another comment made in many institutions was the importance of the ability to expand some areas of work. As was pointed out at one university, it was more than just increasing the number of students – the ability to hire extra staff broadened the department's expertise in teaching and research and enhanced quality by reducing the average administrative load per member of staff. Unlike the other initiatives being considered, staff appointments made on ETP money were 'established posts' rather than fixed-term contracts. The initiative provided for 'focused expansion' and created 'protected departments' at a time when the rest of the university was having to make cuts. While this 'does not necessarily make for happy relationships with the rest of the university, it had a very positive impact on the departments involved in the initiative'. Another senior university manager felt that the expansion of the Engineering department was important, but had some reservations about further expansion. The department was felt to be 'better now that it is bigger but it is not clear that it would continue to get better if it got much bigger'.

The wider impact of the ETP programme in universities and polytechnics was related to the importance of engineering to the overall strategy of the institution. Where Engineering or Computer Science was already a major area of work, ETP was a welcome source of extra funds which may have had important spin-offs for the departments involved, but it did not seem to have had a significant impact across the institution, especially if the extra students were being added to already existing courses.

In one university, members of the Engineering department believed that some of the earmarked money was 'filtered away' since there was a delay in appointing some of the staff, and the recurrent income was not 'carried forward' to the next academic year. It was thought that the extra income had been used to help the university 'balance its books'. In contrast, at another university the central administration had been very keen to expand computer science and electronics, and believed that the initiative allowed them to change the character of the university, which had previously been known mainly for its work in humanities and social sciences. The expansion of information technology was clearly articulated in the university's academic strategy, but it was ETP that really made it possible – putting electronics 'on the map' and allowing for a new building in a period of financial stringency.

Central administrators in another university also stressed the importance of the expansion of Engineering and Technology to the university's own priorities. The cuts in funding and the freezing of posts before the ETP was launched meant that the age structure of academic staff was becoming unbalanced. Regular recruitment is particularly important in fast-moving, technological subjects which need to be constantly infused with 'new blood'. ETP allowed this problem to be addressed by providing additional posts. The younger staff recruited have provided specialist expertise in new areas and 'in some cases have revolutionised the teaching of obsolescent courses'.

In contrast to ETP the EHE projects were required to have an identifiable management structure of their own. Each institution has a central committee to oversee the EHE programme. Sometimes, there is a two-tier structure, with a committee of Council to oversee the broad policy directions and a Management Committee with operational responsibilities.

In most institutions, an EHE director was appointed: in one university no fewer than three full-time enterprise development officers were appointed. In other places a more decentralised mode of operation is being used, with faculty or department staff being designated as EHE tutors. In some cases departmental Enterprise Tutors are given teaching remission. But both the centralized model of implementation and the more devolved model involve the establishment of an Enterprise Unit within the university or polytechnic.

Management structures and styles influence institutional approaches to the Initiative. In institutions where faculties or departments are strong, central academic planning tends to be weak and the interdisciplinary nature of the Initiative caused some initial problems. One university proposed a scheme that would involve only four of seven faculties, but the lead departments would spread the scheme to other departments in later stages.

Most institutions have developed ways in which their experience can be disseminated, both internally and externally. An institutional Enterprise Newsletter is quite common and a number of regional consortia have been established to share experiences of EHE and to join in publicity efforts. Some institutions are hoping to market the expertise they are developing on the basis of their EHE experience.

The way that IRCs are managed and the way that universities manage IRCs are separate, though related issues. The effect on management within a university depends on whether it is a prime or a secondary contractor. Secondary contractors may second staff to the prime contractor, in which case they receive financial reimbursement if the seconded staff member is UFC funded. However, the Research Council pays only what is thought to be the research percentage of their salary costs: the rest is deemed to be met out of the UFC grant. As with other research awards non-UFC staff are funded directly by the IRC, which means that any such staff are lost to the secondary contractor.

Inadequate funding of IRCs is a problem for the prime contractors. One Vice-Chancellor took the view that although for reasons of institutional self esteem and image it was necessary to bid for several IRCs and he was delighted that one of their bids was successful 'two IRCs would have been a cause for concern and three a disaster'.

Some secondary contractors expressed concern that they were being squeezed out by the prime contractor. At one institution they complained that they were involved in only a small part of the project and that they had no control over the IRCs management which was 'run remotely, not by collaboration'. One prime contractor's stated intention was to bring the staff and work to the central facilities. Staff working on the project would work there either temporarily or, if required by the project, permanently. If they worked permanently they would eventually be absorbed on to the host university's full-time staff.

Where the university is a prime contractor, the IRC is usually treated, for management purposes, as though it were an academic department. The Director is accountable to the host university and belongs to relevant university committees. Research grant income, apart from the IRC grant and research contract income are treated in the same way as for departments. Since the university receives only about 40 per cent of the salary costs of UFC funded staff from the Research Council those members of staff are in principle expected to bear a normal teaching load in their teaching departments. In one case where research income to some departments had fallen as a consequence of the establishment of an IRC the university had temporarily suspended its grant allocation formula to allow for compensation to the departments affected.

The internal management of IRCs is obviously affected by the host university's existing structures and procedures and how IRC directors see their roles. In one case the Director had appointed a high level manager so as to leave himself free to oversee the strategic development of the IRC. The desired qualities of the Director were described in another as:

> academic leadership and financial wizardry; liaison with industry, other departments in the University, other universities, research institutes elsewhere; and, above all, the most difficult task, to bring in and enrol all these different sorts of people and co-ordinate their efforts. Someone who is partly academic with some research experience is very important. Also with industrial experience and understanding of how things are done in industry (really obscure to people like myself). Both kinds of experience would be ideal. We hope that someone with appropriate qualifications comes forward.

Although the Director has very considerable management responsibilities most universities have established supporting structures. In this sense they may be said to be treated differently from normal academic departments. One scheme consists of a Management Committee comprising the Director, eight academics, an industrial representative and an administrator. The Committee's role is:

  (i) to review and advise on the progress of the scientific programme;

 (ii) to ensure that the core budget is effectively deployed to enable the scientific programme to advance;

(iii) to approve grant applications and renewals which arise as the programme advances and involve the use of the IRC facilities;

(iv) to liaise with industry and with teaching departments;
 (v) to stimulate collaboration between the IRC and other UK based research groups in universities and in industry;
(vi) to report to SERC and the (university) as required.

In addition, three outstanding scientists with internationally recognized reputations in the appropriate fields have been appointed as external assessors. Their tasks are:

 (i) To visit the IRC annually;
(ii) To review and advise on the development and management of the scientific programme.

Commercial firms have provided substantial sums to IRCs, several hundreds of thousand pounds in some cases. In one institution industry had offered as much financial support as the Research Council; in another more than a one-third of the financial input. Such support is provided in several ways though so far, for obvious reasons at a time when the IRCs are establishing themselves, it is principally for capital spending rather than staffing. There was also some evidence of firms sharing facilities with IRCs. The intellectual property rights (IPRs) associated with industrial links is a concern to some but few general agreements have yet been worked out. At present commercial firms appear to be content with providing support without too many strings attached. No one we interviewed considered that the 'integrity' of their research activities had been undermined by the need to secure financial backing from industry. However, most people associated with IRCs believe that the level of industrial support will increase and, in some cases, it is expected when research council core support comes to an end industry will take over. At that stage industry may well begin to expect some 'return' for its investment and IRCs may need to take this into account in formulating their research programmes.

The general conclusion of this review of management arrangements associated with the four financial initiatives being considered is that universities and polytechnics have absorbed them into existing management structures, but that there have been strains. These are mainly of two kinds. One is dealing with a situation, in institutions which pride themselves on their autonomy, in which an outside piper wants to have some say in the tunes being played; the other is the establishment of appropriate employment conditions and opportunities for career development for staff employed on the basis of what the universities and polytechnics see as short-term funding.

Effects on teaching and research

Nearly all institutions experienced significant increases in the quantity and range of research in departments or centres involved in the Alvey programme. Several reported increases in the number of published articles in refereed journals. In addition to widening the range of academic research, the programme led to an increase in industrial collaboration, which requires 'a degree of additional discipline'.

Most academic participants could point to the spin-offs from industry contacts in terms of further research contracts, visiting staff from companies and use of equipment. There were, however, differing views of its effect on fundamental research. In a high technology area collaboration with industry may be required even for fundamental research. Staff in one university stressed the importance of the Alvey programme in allowing some basic research, even though it had a strong applied focus. In another the laboratory set up with Alvey support has been able to concentrate very effectively upon basic research. The professor thought that the classical pattern of initial basic research, followed by a research programme and then a development and production phase is rarely followed in practice. 'Normally a "bottle-neck" occurs, where a university researcher can step and dig deeper'.

Even this professor, however, worried lest contact with industry should 'be allowed to soak up all your energies', and staff in several other institutions had stronger misgivings about the impact of the Alvey programme on their basic research work. One head of department claimed that 'British industry operates very near the market place' and there has been a tendency for universities to do less fundamental work in order to meet deadlines. He would have moved research to more fundamental levels had it not been for the Alvey programme. Another university saw research being shifted in an applied direction and while this was not bad in itself, basic research was seen as inadequately funded and difficult to support.

While the Alvey Programme was primarily concerned with research, most institutions were able to report some benefits to their teaching, particularly from collaboration with industry. Participation in the Alvey programme was seen by one polytechnic as having been very important for teaching, since 'the development of new research areas gave the department a real shot in the arm' through the addition of six dedicated staff. 'Without Alvey six or seven current courses would not have been developed.' Staff in one university stressed the benefits of being at the 'sharp edge' of pioneering work, which broadened the expertise of staff and provided topics for research students.

In another university, the extra staff were felt to be crucial, since turnover is always very high in computing and in another, research fellows from Alvey projects ran lecture courses and gave individual lectures, as well as supervising research students. In a university with two different projects, one 'made a real contribution to final year modules in computing and related subjects, and provided materials for postgraduate research students'. The other had much less contact with teaching, because it was undertaken not by senior academic staff but by research workers on short-term contracts who felt isolated from the rest of the department. They were effectively an independent entrepreneurial group, which caused some tension and problems, since they felt patronized by regular staff and had considerably less favourable working conditions. In another university a lecturer agreed about the general benefit of 'being involved in state of the art research', but felt there was little direct impact on teaching, other than giving students a working context in which to do their research.

In general where Alvey projects were not integrated with the general work of departments the general view was that staff had had to take time away from teaching duties. One head of department reported that Alvey projects reduced the time available to staff for teaching and, as a result, effective student–staff ratios had gone up. Other universities reported that senior staff had less time to give to students.

However, Alvey projects also contributed equipment which could sometimes be used for teaching. In a field where expensive equipment needs constant updating, the ability to acquire equipment can be crucial to teaching as well as research. At one polytechnic which runs a masters degree and postgraduate diploma in computer science, teaching on these courses was linked to the Alvey research and could use the same equipment. A number of universities also stressed the important benefits of acquiring equipment especially for final year students' projects. One university reported that Alvey projects had spin-offs in terms of CASE awards to students funded by industrial collaborators.

In addition to the increases in numbers of students and staff, the ETP programme made qualitative contributions to both research and teaching. In over half the institutions useful spin-offs to their teaching and research programmes were reported from the extra resources and contacts with industry. Some institutions reported that new teaching methods were developed when courses were developed with the participation of industrial sponsors. In one university a new kind of course was developed based on a 'professional environment' consisting of simulated commercial activities. 'Students have materials taken to them and don't go to lectures, but are doing business on a 7.30a.m. to 9.30p.m. basis – a very different way of approaching the subject which is working out very well.' In another university the improvement in the quality of teaching and research was emphasized because of additional facilities, particularly as regards support for student projects. Staff in a polytechnic reported that ETP enabled them to offer a new option on their robotics course, which introduced interdisciplinary programmes with other departments, stimulating teaching and research in other areas as well. In another polytechnic the initiative was very helpful in allowing the development of two new conversion courses 'for which there is considerable demand'.

In one university department ETP had 'moved the centre of gravity of the department towards Information Engineering, Electronic Engineering and Computer Science'. The injection of additional funds for equipment has meant that the use of computing in teaching has increased substantially.

Engineers in another university which found it difficult to develop its two new courses under the tight deadlines required, nevertheless agreed that they were valuable additions to their work and, at least as important, the extra staff appointed under ETP considerably boosted the research potential of the department, with research income growing from £400,000 in 1983/84 to £2.5m in 1987/88.

EHE focuses explicitly on teaching. Institutions which are implementing the initiative through a central programme of staff development are tending to focus on the need to change teaching styles throughout the institution. In one university it is proposed that by the end of the 5-year period of funding 60 per cent of its academic staff will have had the opportunity to acquire the skills and competencies of enterprise and enterprise teaching. This will encourage them to adapt the content and processes of their courses so as to develop enterprise in their students. The approach is based on the premise that enterprise skills can be integrated into any subject, and that therefore the aim is to change approaches to learning rather than to introduce new content: what one EHE coordinator saw as a change of culture, rather than the number or kinds of courses available. In some institutions, where an institution wide scheme was proposed, benefits were expected from having different areas of activity working together.

This approach was not without critics. The head of an engineering department, which has an outstanding record of industrial contacts and a generally favourable attitude towards 'enterprise', considered that:

> it is a rather undifferentiated kind of initiative. There is a tendency for training to be provided by trainers from industry and to be concentrated at lower skill levels. The presumption that university staff are out of touch with industry is not true for the engineering department. Many industrialists who come into our department find it a pretty austere and hard working environment . . . on the other hand I can think of faculties where a little pep may be of value . . . It is not obvious to me that enterprise is widespread in industry and that we in universities have to learn it from them.

He felt that the central arrangements for the scheme within the university did not appreciate sufficiently the different needs of different departments.

Other universities and polytechnics tend to see the aims of the Initiative primarily in terms of introducing students to the world of work, so their approach focuses on the needs of employers and is often organized on a more decentralized basis. These institutions are often located in industrial regions; they already have good links with commercial firms and see the Initiative as faculty or discipline based with specific programmes designed to fit the particular needs of employers. While all bids involve employer support, some tend to put a markedly higher priority on the needs of industry and commerce. They stress the amount of time spent establishing contact and securing support from different kinds of employers for the bid.

A third approach is to integrate enterprise courses into regular degree programmes through modular courses. One university was proposing to take advantage of the modular nature of its degree courses and to create opportunities by the end of the 5-year period for all students to undertake one 'enterprise' module as part of their degree programmes. Some of the polytechnics were adopting a similar strategy.

Contrastingly, IRCs are research centres, established to concentrate research, particularly where established disciplines are converging. One important issue is whether this concentration of research will have a detrimental effect on university teaching. One academic scientist expressed the fear that:

> the creation of IRCs, will damage teaching since university departments should be the 'ideas factory' which stimulate creativity among research students and, ultimately undergraduates. Research in a university department often has freshness and immediacy, as a result of contact with the best students which 'isolated' IRCs will lack; they may become 'fossilized' because of their separation from mainstream university activities.

If research and teaching are complementary, any development that stimulates one ought, in principle, to benefit the other. If an innovation has the effect of separating them geographically, organizationally, or academically or if staff doing research *and* teaching increase the proportion of their time devoted to research, there is a point beyond which teaching must suffer. Furthermore if the activities are really complementary, there may be an adverse effect on research itself because it will no longer have teaching to feed on. However, unless teaching and research are linearly complementary some combinations of teaching and research will yield a higher total academic 'output' than others.

One benefit to teaching for the prime contractors is the capacity to attract the most promising academics in a field. However, against this there are the effects on teaching and research in other universities and polytechnics. Financial stringency may prevent institutions from replacing academic staff lost to IRCs. This is thought to be particularly serious for the coverage of specialist areas in teaching programmes. A widely held view is that the only area of teaching where there are unequivocal gains is research training in the field covered by IRCs.

The view of the effect on research in institutions not receiving IRC funds was also divided. On the one hand, there was the expectation that these institutions would become research backwaters attracting neither research grants nor research studentships. On the other hand, a number of institutions claim to have received Research Council support because their bids had impressed the Research Councils, though not sufficiently to be awarded the IRC. There was also uncertainty about the effect of IRCs on non-IRC fields within a university. It was thought that the morale of staff would be lowered if it was believed that less money was available for non-IRC activities which would mean equipment becoming obsolete and contract research staff fewer.

There are widely different views about the relative advantages and disadvantages of a small number of large research groups compared with a large number of small groups. One view was that the reduction in support for small-scale research that would result from IRCs would be detrimental: 'the really important discoveries are made by small groups of workers operating as individuals, rather than by huge conglomerations of maybe a hundred people'. Sceptics also claimed that IRCs may become 'isolated'. Lacking the immediacy of contact with students and other academics indirectly involved in their areas of research they may become 'fossilized'. Conversely better conditions of employment for research staff which are more likely in larger groups are generally welcomed. One comment was that longer term contracts have resulted 'in a general feeling of increased confidence in research funding and hence a more confident and enthusiastic approach to the research projects'.

Concluding comments

The four initiatives discussed in this chapter have had very different objectives with regard to teaching and research. In broad terms two, ETP and EHE, were intended primarily to affect teaching while Alvey and IRCs are concerned primarily with research. All, however, with the possible exception of the EHE which, so far at least is confined to undergraduate teaching, have had some effects on both the teaching and research of universities and polytechnics through four main mechanisms. The first is simply the additional resources. At a time of severe financial stringency, the purchase of equipment and the recruitment of new staff permitted many activities that would not have been possible otherwise. The second is the effect of encouraging institutions, or groups of individuals within them to share expertise in order to prepare bids. The third results from the requirement in all the programmes for collaboration with industrial and commercial organizations. This has resulted in new ideas, which most academics involved have appreciated, and additional resources which they have appreciated even more. The fourth, where the effects are much more varied arise from spin-offs within higher education institutions where the presence of active researchers is used to enhance teaching programmes or, particularly in the case of ETP, where the recruitment of additional staff for teaching enabled some institutions to build up a research capacity they did not have previously. The experience here is varied because it was not unusual in the Alvey programme for research groups to be virtually isolated from the rest of the institution and the effect of some of the IRCs may be to separate research and teaching quite sharply.

Overall the case studies show that the four initiatives have had a marked effect on higher education institutions that extends well beyond the small percentage of recurrent funding that they accounted for. Many of the changes have been perceived as benefits by those who were, or are actively involved in them. They have certainly been instrumental in bringing about substantial change in British higher education. A considerable number of specific gains have been identified. Nearly all the institutions involved in the ETP programme felt that it had a positive overall impact on the academic work of the departments involved, and in many cases on the institution as a whole. Alvey was widely believed to have played a significant part in building up strong Information Technology departments and criticized mainly for having come to an end. Both EHE and IRCs were too recent for this kind of overall judgement but both had far more supporters than critics.

There appears to be little concern, even in universities, that the new funding mechanisms represent a serious infringement on institutional autonomy. For example in none of the case study institutions undertaking EHE initiatives was there any serious concern amongst senior staff about this issue. It was felt that these were activities in keeping with the academic mission of the institution, and that once the contract had been negotiated the monitoring and evaluation were legitimate accountability. Even the arguments about intellectual property rights in the Alvey and IRC programmes seem to have been more concerned with who has control of any cash generated than with issues of principle about open publication of research findings.

We cannot claim to have sampled a representative cross-section of university opinion in this respect, and there certainly are worries about whether for example market approaches to funding are resulting in serious damage to quality of both teaching and research. Most of our respondents stood to gain from the initiatives in one way or another. However, it does appear that the debate about academic autonomy has in practice moved beyond simplistic claims that academics need to be responsible only to their professional consciences and their academic peers.

Against the gains some problems have been identified. The most explicit of these are the time and resources used in preparing bids for funds. An important issue here is the probability of success, or the proportion of wasted bids in relation to what is required to make a convincing bid. The European Community ESPRIT programme, which in some respects is a successor to Alvey, was felt to cost much more to bid for and to have much lower chances of success for bids. One university was told that the project for which they bid was oversubscribed by a factor of ten. Considering the time and effort involved in preparing bids, they felt competitive bidding on these terms represents a 'step backwards' in European research. Other universities were concerned about the costs of building up new collaborative groups with partners in Europe. One university professor had made at least a dozen trips to Europe within the previous year. Since ESPRIT requires more collaborators (a typical group is much bigger as well as being international), it takes more resources to prepare a convincing bid than Alvey did.

In general enforced collaboration generates a mixed reaction. While some dispersed research teams work well, it is more usual to find attitudes that treat collaboration as at best an excuse for some interesting travel and at worst a chore, particularly the process of building up inter-institutional research teams. In particular collaboration between institutions in the establishment of IRCs in most cases does not appear to have been very successful.

Other possible losses arise from the short term nature of such initiatives. The Alvey programme, for example, built up some strong research teams, many of which had to be dismantled when the funding came to an end. One university professor claimed that a 'stop–go' policy of government support is almost worse than no policy at all. He hoped that future programmes would avoid sudden discontinuities, either upwards or downwards. Sudden increases in funding lead to recruitment problems and, while there should be a mechanism for weeding out unsuccessful groups, sudden curtailment is not a very efficient way of doing this:

> If you suddenly get Alvey and 5 years later the IED [Information Engineering Directorate of the Department of Trade and Industry] proposals, and in between that every 3 years ESPRIT, with specified research targets and new rules for collaboration, a great deal of resource and energy is wasted restructuring groups and reformulating research proposals to match the latest fashion, which is not a good way of doing research.

Several finance officers expressed the concern that EHE is 'yet another short-term initiative that does not cover its full costs'. There was also some doubt about whether the undoubted goodwill from industrial partners would be translated into resources.

The most fundamental question for the present study is whether equivalent benefits could have been obtained if similar funding had been allocated under earlier, less rigidly specified mechanisms, in particular if the resources devoted to bidding had been used directly for teaching and research. This kind of question is impossible to answer. Many of the respondents to our surveys claimed that the effects of the initiatives was to permit them to undertake activities they wanted to do anyway. However, while certain individuals may have wanted to do what the EHE, for example, has permitted them to do, it is not at all clear that their institution's decision-making machinery would have permitted them to do it without the nudge from outside.

Intuitively and on the basis of previous experience of innovation in higher education, it seems unlikely that the addition of an extra three per cent to the general subsidy to higher education institutions would have achieved similar results in bringing about change, and our estimates that even in the worst case no more than seven per cent of the institutional income derived from an initiative was spent in bidding do not seem to lend much support to claims that bidding costs were excessive in the case of the four programmes examined in this chapter.

9

The British Experience in an International Context[*]

Introduction

Britain was not the only country to have experienced changes in the funding of higher education during the 1980s: a recent international study (Williams, 1990) shows similar developments in many others.

In nearly all the countries included in the study there is discussion of, and experimentation with, new funding mechanisms. Reforms that are underway or being discussed include:

1. Changes in the proportions of central and local government finance.
2. New mechanisms of central government resource allocation.
3. Increased contributions from ministries other than the Ministry of Education.
4. Increased sophistication of formulae used in determining the allocations to each institution.
5. Greater financial autonomy for the institutions once they have received their funds.
6. Increased proportion of income from student fees.
7. Sharper distinction between funding of research and of teaching.
8. Increased proportion of public funding for defined activities in the institutions.
9. Larger share of income coming from contracts with employers and commercial organizations.

Many governments now see financial incentives as being more effective than administrative intervention in influencing patterns of academic activity. They are showing an interest in the introduction of market mechanisms and incentives in the funding of higher education institutions. Public funding agencies are becoming increasingly selective, in several countries taking the form of 'buying' services from higher education; and

[*] This chapter is derived largely from the OECD report and the ten country case studies, listed in its bibliography, which support it. Quotations are from the case studies unless otherwise indicated.

universities and colleges are being encouraged to seek an increasing proportion of their finance from non-traditional sources.

However, in all the countries which participated in the OECD study, except Japan, where exactly half of total institutional income in 1985 came from private sources, the main source of finance for higher education remains public funds. In Germany, the USA and Canada this means principally the individual Lander, States, or Provinces; while elsewhere national governments are the dominant source of funds.

Japan and the USA

In the USA, there are broadly two models of higher education funding; one for state supported or 'public' colleges and universities, and the other for private or 'independent' colleges and universities. In 1984/85 6.7 million out of a total enrolment of 9.0 million students were in the 'public sector'; that is, almost exactly 75 per cent. However, the private institutions had 35 per cent of total expenditure giving an average recurrent expenditure per full-time equivalent student of $11,200 compared with $7,001 in public universities. The pattern of income of the two sectors is markedly different: 39 per cent of the income of private universities in 1984/85 came from student tuition fees compared with 15 per cent in the public institutions. Conversely, over 45 per cent of the income of the public universities came from state governments compared with less than 2 per cent in the private sector. The other major difference is in endowment income and private gifts: 9 per cent of private sector income compared with only 3 per cent in the public sector came from this source.

The patterns have changed significantly since 1970. In particular there has been a big increase in income from sales of services and, in both sectors, a decline in the proportion of income received directly from the Federal Government. However, this last needs to be treated with caution; there has been a shift towards subsidization of the fees and living costs of individual students rather than a reduction in the total Federal share of higher education funding.

The differences between the public and private sectors in Japan are greater than in the USA. In 1987, 63 per cent of the income of National Universities came from the government and 9 per cent from tuition fees. Of the remainder, most was income of hospitals attached to universities. In the private sector 63 per cent came in the form of tuition fees and 14 per cent from the 'current cost subsidy' of the central government. Neither public nor private institutions yet obtain any significant income from the sale of educational or research services, but the government has recently made legal changes to permit National Universities to increase their income from such sources.

The other major contrast with the USA is in expenditure per student, which in Japan is much higher in the public than in the private institutions – $10,258 compared with $5,212 in 1985. This disparity is largely a result of the differences in the mix of subjects taught in the two sectors. The National institutions have a high proportion of their students in Natural Sciences, Engineering, and Education, the private institutions tend to have most of their students in Humanities, Social Sciences and Home Economics.

Japan and the USA thus present two contrasting models of the role of public funding. In the USA the public sector provides a floor of basic facilities to most students at reasonable public and private costs. Students who wish for something different, for example, a collegial atmosphere, or a more favourable staff student ratio, or an education based on a particular religion pay for the privilege, often very heavily. Competition for entry is most intense in the top-quality private universities. In Japan, on the other hand, the role of public funding is to provide high-quality education in the most expensive subjects to the most able students. Competition for such institutions is very severe. Meanwhile the majority of students attend private universities with much less favourable facilities and staffing, and virtually the full cost of their education is borne by their families.

In Japan as in the USA there are differences between the National Universities and the private institutions in funding *mechanisms*. The former are largely funded through the National Schools Special Account which is an administrative agency responsible for the financial administration of the universities. Special accounts in Japanese law are able to retain income they earn from user charges, but any such income belongs to the account as a whole not the institution which earns it so there is little incentive for individual institutions to make efforts to raise additional income.

More than two-thirds of the income of private Japanese institutions comes from fees and other student charges. However, since 1970 they have received a 'current costs subsidy' from Central Government. They share a formula-based grant linked largely to student enrolment weighted by standard cost estimates and the priority attached by government to different subjects. This is deemed to 'function as an incentive system to encourage changes desired by the Ministry of Education' (Williams, 1990).

In Finland and the Netherlands and some other countries private universities have effectively been absorbed into the public sector. The opposite and much more recent trend in several countries, is for private universities to develop in response to market opportunities and perceived gaps in public sector provision. The trend towards private institutions, which form a small proportion of the total provision, except in Japan and the USA, seems likely to increase in importance in the future as public institutions come to depend more on private funds and market oriented funding mechanism. In several countries, public agencies make funds available to private institutions through a variety of routes.

Formulae and contracts

The most widespread change in funding mechanisms in European OECD countries is the increasing use, and increasing complexity of formula funding. Most governments have until recently used some form of incremental funding which was unproblematic when higher education systems were expanding, but is almost impossible to implement rationally if resources are not growing. There is no reason in principle why increments should not be negative but in practice a negative increment means that some activities have to be discontinued or reduced in volume and this is resisted by groups whose resources are cut. This creates difficult management problems for the institutions, and funding agencies in several countries have shown impatience with the capacity of institutional managers to make such hard choices. One possibility is for funding bodies to impose equal cuts on all activities but to reinstate part of the resources by allowing institutions to bid for funds for specific innovations. Various versions of this arrangement have been adopted in several countries during the past 10 years.

Recent reforms of funding mechanisms in Denmark and the Netherlands provide examples of the use of formulae to yield sophisticated incentive systems for the universities. They represent ways of reconciling legitimate government concern to determine major priorities in the use of public funds with the equally legitimate demands of academic institutions to be able to carry out their teaching and research functions according to academic and professional judgements.

In Denmark, the 'budgets are split into activity areas. By using a very fine meshed division the central budget agency gets a fairly great influence on the budget of individual institutions . . . it becomes possible for the central authorities to make considerable resource related priority decisions between the subject areas of the institutions'. An interesting feature of the model is that resources are linked not only to the number of students but to the number of students completing courses. This encourages universities to graduate as many students as possible as quickly as possible: an important efficiency issue in a country where it is common for students to take 5 or more years to graduate.

The basic allocation is supplemented by a 'pool' which enables the Ministry to support selective new initiatives against a background of financial stringency. The government can spread its basic allocation amongst all institutions according to standard criteria or formulae while at the same time having some funds which can be used selectively to bring about changes in accordance with government priorities. The pool consists of about 1 per cent of total recurrent expenditure which is held back from the initial formula-based allocation and which can be claimed by the institutions as grants for new initiatives.

In the Netherlands funding consists essentially of formula-based block grants. 'However, the amount of funds is not based simply on enrolment. In addition, every drop-out as well as every graduate contributes to the institution's formula based grant.' Thus the resources formulae provide incentives for prompt identification of potential drop-outs as well as the stimulation of rapid graduation.

The use of formulae is facilitated by the rapid development of computerized management models. However, in developing sophisticated formulae one problem, referred to in both the Netherlands and the Danish reports, is that it is not always effective to increase the complexity of formulae since complexity may distort the signals that the formulae are intended to convey.

Conceptually, contracting has much in common with formula funding. Formulae are in effect the specifications of what the funding agencies want, and the institutions are able to obtain funds to the extent that they meet these specifications. There are, however, two important differences. One is that formulae are usually applied retrospectively: institutions are paid on the basis of previous student numbers, whereas contract systems take future commitments as the main basis of funding allocations. The other difference is that formulae are normally open-ended standard price contracts. Institutions are funded at a fixed price according to the number of students they recruit. Contracting usually requires an individual negotiation of some sort on both numbers and price and is also often a competitive zero sum game, because total public funding for higher education is determined by government before contract negotiations take place.

In Australia a form of contracting is in operation. From 1989 universities and colleges have been funded according to their mix of activities. Educational profiles have been introduced to allow each institution to develop in the way that best fits its particular mission and objectives. Institutions negotiate with the Federal Government to reach an agreed profile which provides a basis for determining the resources needed by them to achieve their mission and objectives. In addition, universities and colleges are encouraged to earn income from other sources for research and consultancy.

French universities have had legal independence since the 1960s and each has its own budget. A policy of contractual funding is in operation. Each institution defines its policy; and a 4-year contract covering the whole of its activities is agreed with the Ministry. The objective is 'to increase institutional autonomy while permitting the state to carry out more effectively its responsibilities of regulating and co-ordinating the university system'. Financial autonomy has also been increased with respect to externally generated funds largely in order to provide an incentive for them to earn money from external sources.

Fees

Several countries are introducing, or considering the introduction of, some form of 'cost recovery' from students. Supporters of fees claim that they:

(a) increase the total resources available to higher education;
(b) enhance institutional autonomy;

(c) improve efficiency;
(d) give power to students as consumers to influence the orientation of higher education.

It is important to note that (b) and (c) and to some extent (d) are about financial mechanisms, not sources of funds. Fee income is free income in the sense that it is not subject to government contracts or formulae. From the point of view of institutional efficiency and autonomy it matters little whether the fees are paid by the students out of their own resources or whether the students merely act as a channel for the transfer of public funds to the universities. Many of the student aid schemes in the USA are essentially a means of transferring Federal funds to higher education institutions in a country where the Constitution prohibits direct Federal intervention in education.

Most countries in Continental Europe have a long tradition of charging no fees or very low ones for students on Initial Courses. But in most, students attending courses of Continuing or Recurrent Education, or their employers, are required to pay fees covering the full cost of the courses. OECD countries in which significant fees are actually paid by students on regular courses, are Japan, Spain, the USA and the Netherlands. In Japan fees accounted for 36 per cent of the income of all higher education institutions in 1985 and there was only a small amount of public subsidy of them. In the USA fees accounted for 23 per cent of institutional income but a significant part of this was subsidized through loan and grant schemes. In Spain 20 per cent of the income of universities came from student fees and there was little public subsidy. In the Netherlands students pay fees amounting to about 12 per cent of university income, but this is supported by grants and loans.

Australia has introduced a Higher Education Contribution Scheme whereby students contribute about 20 per cent of the costs of their higher education. They can pay their contribution directly to the institution on enrolment each semester. However, the most novel aspect of the scheme is that students can choose to have their contribution collected through the taxation system after they enter employment, with no payment required until their personal taxable income reaches the level of the average earnings of all Australians. The amount they contribute depends upon the subjects and number of study units they undertake each semester, and is payable whether they pass or fail. Once they have paid their contributions they have no further liability, so although the repayments are collected through the tax system it is not strictly speaking a graduate tax.

The concept of financing higher education through vouchers underlies the Danish 'clip-card' system. The card is a book of vouchers each entitling the student to 1 month of study, but it is flexible in that within broad limits students are able to use their entitlements when it is most convenient to them. Each eligible student can obtain a card divided into 48 monthly 'clips' and for each month of study undertaken one 'clip' is used up. Any unused portion of the card can be retained for later use. Beyond the basic 4 years of undergraduate study students are able to apply for an advanced card but the clipping on this is designed in such a way as to provide an incentive for students to complete their courses quickly.

Research and other services

In most OECD countries a considerable amount of university research has traditionally been funded outside the general university budget, but there are big differences between countries. At one extreme, in Japan specific research grants amount to only 3 per cent of the total national expenditure on higher education institutions. (Though in addition to expenditure on higher education institutions the Ministry of Science, Education and Culture spends considerably more on specialized research institutes that are not considered to be part of the higher education system.)

In several other countries over 10 per cent of university income comes in the form of research grants. In Finland research funds, amounting to 11 per cent of university income, were provided by the Academy of Finland and the Ministries of Trade, Environment and Labour in 1987. In Norway in 1987 about 6 per cent of the income of higher education institutions consisted of research grants from the Norwegian Research Council and about 4 per cent research grants from private agencies. In the USA just over 10 per cent of the total income of higher education in 1984/85 was in the form of research grants and contracts from Federal and State governments and another 5 per cent came from private gifts, grants and contracts. In Germany about 12 per cent of recurrent funding of institutions is in the form of specific grants and contracts (a further 25 per cent consists of revenues from hospitals associated with the universities). In France, apart from research contracts and government remuneration of academic and research staff, university research has two main supplementary sources of funding. The first is the Higher Education Ministry which provides research funds of which about two-thirds are included in the quadrennial research contracts, and the second is major research organizations, in particular the National Centre for Scientific Research, which funds research centres associated with universities.

Income from the sale of other academic services is only a small part of the income of higher education institutions in most countries, but it has attracted much attention and concern. The majority of the countries that took part in the OECD study have experienced a significant increase in both the amount and the proportion of income from such sources, though usually from a very low base. Many have taken steps in recent years to make it easier for higher education institutions to earn revenue by selling their services. Comparisons of the amounts involved are difficult because of different statistical definitions and financial accounting practices.

In German universities such income is known as third party funds. They are held in special accounts on behalf of the professors who are responsible for the research. Income from such activities increased by 50 per cent in real terms between 1970 and 1985 and accounted in total for about a quarter of the resources of higher education institutions in the late 1980s. The contribution from industry was about 2 per cent of the total.

In the Netherlands the so-called third flow of funds corresponding broadly to the sale of services amounted to about 8 per cent of the total in the mid-1980s. In Denmark where there was until very recently little funding of higher education from outside government, the 'traditional system of finance is being supplemented by the growth and increasing use of new sources of finance and new structures of finance. So far the most important element in this has been the set of rules governing the sale of services to the outside which breaks the main principle in the public budget and appropriation system which is that expenses and income are to be paid to the Treasury and cannot be used by the institutions. The new rules make it possible for the institutions to extend their traditional activities or to commence new ones such as [full cost] courses and consultancy activities.'

Universities in Finland have also begun to earn income from a wide range of non-traditional activities: 'The growing demands for contract research and other expert services have brought various technology centres and villages into university towns. The institutions are involved in this activity as shareholders. Some institutions of higher education have founded scientific business enterprises, because these offer more flexible financing and bookkeeping than those of the decision-making organizations in the institutions themselves. These firms sell research and other expert services. . . . This type of activity which allows the universities to make a more flexible use of their funds will probably grow in the future.'

In France 'one of the striking developments of recent years has been the growth of higher education funding by local communities, in particular in the form of building costs to encourage the establishment of new institutions in the locality'. There has also been a growth of funding from industry and commerce and the establishment of commercial enterprises by universities which were legalized by the Higher Education Law of 1984. One of the main aims is to provide more management flexibility than is possible in universities that are closely regulated by public authorities. By the beginning of 1988 about 25 such enterprises had been registered. Most were concerned with some aspect of high technology although some undertake commercial business management consultancy.

In Japan, where public universities have little control over their own budgets, there have been debates within government about the desirability of changing the legal status of national universities and transforming them into 'Special Juristic Persons' which would enable them to control their own budgets and to supplement them from appropriate sources. However, so far this proposal has not been accepted, partly on the grounds that the examples of the private universities and colleges show that independent

Table 9.1 Sources of income of higher education institutions in OECD countries

		General		Other income of which from:	
	Year	*Public funds (%)*	*Fees (%)*	*Industry (%)*	*Other (%)*
Australia	1987	88	2	0.1	10
Finland, public institutions	1987	85	–	4	11
France, all institutions	1975	93	3	2	4
	1984	89	4	–	6
Germany, all higher education	1986	68	0	3	25
Japan:					
Private 4-year institutions	1971	9	76	–	15
	1985	15	65	–	20
Public institutions	1970	83	2	–	15
	1987	63	9	3	25
All institutions	1971	53	32	–	15
	1985	42	36	–	22
Netherlands, all institutions	1985	80	12	–	8
Norway, public institutions	1975	95	0	–	5
	1987	90	0	2	8
Spain, universities	mid-1980s	80	20	–	–
UK:					
Universities	1970/71	71	6	–	23
	1986/87	55	14	7	28
Polytechnics	1986/87	72	16	3	11
USA:					
Private institutions	1969/70	21	39	–	40
	1984/85	18	39	11	32
Public institutions	1969/70	61	15	–	24
	1984/85	59	14	6	20
All institutions	1969/70	47	21	–	32
	1986	45	22	8	25

Source: *Financing Higher Education: Current Patterns* (OECD, 1990).
Australia: Industry figure from Higher Education Grants and Finance Branch DEET, Canberra July 1991.
Finland: Norway: Figures for fees not available but very small.
France: Expenditure of National Ministry of Education.
Germany: The figure for funding from industry comes from a paper by K. Alewell (Giessen University), *Public Finance and Institutional Autonomy* (1991) (Unpublished observations).
Japan: 73 per cent of other income is revenue of attached hospitals.
UK: Almost all the fees of UK undergraduate students are paid out of public funds. This amounts to about half the fee income of universities and probably a greater proportion of the fee income of polytechnics. Figures for industry income from Williams and Loder (1992).
USA: Figures include all government expenditure at all levels. Loans and grants to students amounted to about 80 per cent of fees in 1969/70 and 95 per cent in 1984/5.

status does not necessarily induce organizational efficiency or vitality. Meanwhile the Ministry of Education, Science and Culture can create special finance codes which permit research grants and contracts from private businesses to be put into special accounts rather like the German Third Party Funds. There was a steady increase in funds during the 1980s but in 1985 they still accounted for less than 4 per cent of the total income of higher education institutions. It is also possible for a national institution to establish an 'attached foundation' which 'typically established upon contributions from private corporations and the alumni, would contribute to academic activities not supported by official budgets.'

In the USA where the concept of higher education institutions as economic enterprises selling academic services is much better established than in any other OECD country most institutions have specialist staff concerned with selling the institution and with other forms of fundraising. 'Sales and Services' by higher education institutions (excluding research contracts) already accounted for 17 per cent of their income in 1969/70 and by 1984/85 this had risen to over 21 per cent. There was not a great difference between the public and private institutions. However, these figures include 'revenues generated from . . . such auxiliary enterprises as athletics, student residence facilities, cafeterias, and campus bookstores' which are usually excluded from apparently comparable British figures.

Table 9.1 summarizes the sources of higher education funding in the ten countries that provided information for the OECD study. Of the ten there are six which in the second half of the 1980s the higher education institutions were still receiving 80 per cent or more of their funding in general subsidy from public funds. There were three in which more than 20 per cent of the income came from fees, Japan (36 per cent), USA (22 per cent), Spain (20 per cent). In the USA a high proportion of this fee income was subsidized from public funds.

In conclusion it may be said that though there may have been many changes in the funding of higher education in the 1980s it remained an activity that was overwhelmingly dependent on public funds with the exception of Japan where the public contribution to the private universities and colleges was growing rapidly.

10

Diagnosis and Prognosis

Colleges, bureaucracies and markets

This study has explored a set of higher education establishments in transition from an élite university led system towards the much more varied array of institutions and activities that constitute mass higher education. The Leverhulme Reports of the early 1980s drew attention to the narrow range of courses that were available in British higher education and recommended much greater diversity of provision. The 1980s may therefore be described as the post-Leverhulme period in contrast to the post-Robbins period which lasted from 1964 to 1981. The main characteristic of the earlier period was a university dominated expansion in which governments accepted the principle that 'courses of higher education should be available to all who were qualified by ability and attainment to pursue them and who wanted to do so', and they funded the expected demand by traditionally qualified school leavers for places on honours degree courses, broadly on an average cost basis. The main characteristic of the post-Leverhulme period was expansion of student numbers outside the universities and much greater variety of provision and funding.

During the great expansion of higher education that followed the end of the Second World War, and continued up to the early 1970s, it was widely accepted – on grounds of both equity and efficiency – that only public funds could provide the resources needed. There was a general shift away from private funding and more and more institutions and students came to a greater and greater extent under the umbrella of state funding. By the mid-1970s the idea of higher education as a publicly provided service was overwhelmingly the dominant model.

In the 1980s there was a remarkable reversal of that trend: in large part, undoubtedly, as an aspect of the worldwide retreat of 'the state' as a universal provider of free, or heavily subsidized services. Governments have become much more selective in the criteria by which they allocate funds to higher education institutions; and they have encouraged universities and colleges to seek larger proportions of their funds from non-government sources.

As the previous chapter has shown there has been a growing interest worldwide in the introduction of market incentives and forms of organization. Governments are seeing financial incentives as a more effective way of influencing the pattern of activities in higher education institutions than administrative intervention. Changes in public funding have aimed both to increase the financial autonomy of universities and colleges and to concentrate public funds more sharply on national priorities. In Britain as in some other countries national funding agencies now see themselves as 'buying services' from universities and colleges on a contractual basis, rather than subsidising them.

The traditional case for public funding of higher education was three-fold. One, and in practice the most important in many countries, was the desire by the state to influence and often control an activity that prepared individuals for leading positions in many walks of life. The second was an efficiency argument, much used by economists in the 1960s. In essence this was that the returns to higher education, although considerable, are very uncertain for any individual person. Therefore unless the state, representing all citizens, plays an active part there will be less than a socially optimum amount of investment in higher education. The Robbins Report recommendations for massive expansion in the early 1960s were based essentially on this argument. The Report showed that very large numbers of young people potentially able to benefit from higher education were not doing so, to the detriment of themselves and the nation. Large-scale publicly funded expansion was the remedy proposed; and this was accepted by all governments as the basis of their higher education policies until the early 1980s. The third reason why, in the welfare dominated post-war period, it was taken for granted that the state must play a major part in higher education funding, was equity. Higher education is expensive; and unless it is heavily subsidized, many people will be unable to benefit from it and this is unfair.

However, although there was widespread consensus that the state must play a leading role in funding a mass higher education system, there was, until the 1980s, little discussion, outside the narrow ranks of economists of education, of the form this support should take. Recurrent funding tended to be either incremental or based on detailed line-by-line budgets. In Britain we had both, with the universities receiving largely incrementally determined block grants and the polytechnics and colleges having budgets that were both determined and administered on a rigid line-by-line basis.

Incremental block grants led to highly developed collegial forms of management in British universities. Funds were distributed largely on the basis of consensus amongst providers of academic services, and it was widely claimed by universities that this resulted in efficient internal resource allocation. Any organization where the relationship between inputs and outputs is complex, and which depends on high-level professional skills, performs best if there is some collegial participation in its management procedures. The basic economic truism that 'there is no such thing as a free lunch' is most likely to be recognized by individuals who have some control over their own resources. When resources were plentiful academic criteria dominated resource allocation decisions. The internal dynamic of disciplines and subjects, rather than external economic or social pressures, determined patterns of academic activity. Within institutions there was usually some willingness to compromise since social relationships within universities are more comfortable if the distribution of resources is based on consent. People scratched each other's backs. Consensus is not too difficult to achieve in a time of affluence. If existing activities are all able to survive resource negotiation can focus on prioritizing new proposals.

When a collegial model of resource allocation is working well, there are high academic standards and an ethos of professional integrity. However, this can degenerate into protection of vested interests, particularly when resources are scarce. In particular innovation is difficult. No constituent of the consensus is willing to give anything up especially to a potential new competitor.

Line-by-line budgets stimulate a different kind of management response. Bureaucratic regulation is necessary to ensure that budgets are spent as intended. Tight management structures and bureaucratic administration, can promote efficient resource use and rapid response to a changing environment. Bureaucratic procedures can protect quality, by monitoring resource use and ensuring that they are adequate and used effectively. However, amongst the academic staff there may be a sense of alienation from funding agencies, particularly if there are rigorous systems of external accountability. The funding agency comes to be seen as a black box which, apparently arbitrarily, sometimes accepts claims for additional resources and sometimes does not. Users of funds have little incentive to take much account of overall constraints. Claims for funds are based on claims about the expected *benefits* rather than a comparison of benefits and opportunity *costs*.

An alternative to collegial and bureaucratic forms of resource allocation is the market. Plural sources and mechanisms of funding, their advocates claim, buttress the multiple functions and activities of a modern higher education system. According to market theory the fundamental resource allocation issue is not *what* the priorities are to be but *how* they are to be established. There are four groups who can claim the right to be heard: academics, whose legitimacy comes from expertise; institutional managers, who have a broader, trans-disciplinary academic viewpoint; government, representing the interests of society as a whole; and students and their employers as consumers of academic services. Many different sources of funding and many different criteria for the disbursement of funds may complicate the lives of university managements but according to this view pluralism is the surest guarantee of the capacity of higher education institutions to perform their proper long-term functions. No single set of priorities is dominant and no single criterion determines the resources an institution receives. A university or college with several funding sources, is likely to be active in seeking out funds and to be more genuinely autonomous than one which is dependent on a single funding body.

The case for market approaches to higher education funding is based on three main propositions. One is the belief that the private sector can relieve governments of some of the cost burden. The second is that many of the benefits of higher education accrue to private individuals and they should be prepared to pay for them. However, private finance is not necessary for market mechanisms to operate and the third premise is that both external and internal efficiency improve if government agencies buy services from universities rather than make grants to them. More efficient institutions offering better value for money flourish while those that are less efficient lose out. Markets put the power in the hands of purchasers of higher education services, so the system has to be responsive to their demands. Advocates of markets define efficiency as the satisfaction of consumer wants at minimum costs.

Market systems of finance no less than the two other approaches have both advantages and disadvantages. During the course of our research we heard several expressions of concern about some of the effects of the shift towards market forms of funding.

(a) Basic research and the teaching of fundamentals suffer because they are difficult to justify in terms of short-term market criteria.
(b) Fashion, rather than underlying need plays a significant part in determining which activities prosper and which decline.
(c) Multiple and competitive funding exacerbates disparities between large and prestigious national universities and smaller regional institutions.
(d) Government and commercial research sponsors restrict the publication of new findings, thus endangering traditional academic freedoms and impeding the process of scientific discovery.
(e) Competitive resource allocation results in excessive amounts of academic staff time and other resources being devoted to preparing proposals and accounting for the way in which funds are used. Packaging of teaching and research improves, but at the expense of content.
(f) If the main sources of funds are required to maintain core activities, then the only sources of finance for innovation are the subsidiary providers. This gives them an influence on patterns of the development that is disproportionate in relation to the amount of resources they contribute.
(g) When an academic institution is entirely dependent on a single government agency it may not be genuinely independent but the agency does have some responsibility for the integrity of the institution as a whole. If there are a large number of agencies, each providing a small amount of funds, none has any such responsibility.

Most of the anxieties amount to a concern that too much emphasis on selling educational and research services endangers their quality and that competition endangers both academic freedom and intrinsically valuable teaching, research and scholarship. A shift towards market funding favours consumer perceptions of quality rather than those of the producers who dominate collegial and bureaucratic systems. As far as teaching is concerned this raises the question of whether students are competent judges of quality. If the consumer is deemed to be the individual student there are problems. It is difficult to assess the quality of a course until it is experienced and by then it is usually too late to do much about it. It is certainly possible to overstate the dangers. As the evidence of the overseas student market shows, after the initial excesses, market competition is at least as likely to be on quality as on price. However, a market-dominated system of higher education ought to have independent and reliable sources of advice for potential students and it should be externally and expertly monitored if abuses are to be avoided. Monitoring needs to concentrate particularly on the accuracy and comprehensiveness of promotional information provided to students and other potential clients.

As far as research is concerned there are few problems about the competence of sponsors to judge quality of applied research. There are, however, some dangers, especially in the 'softer' areas of research, where quality judgements are particularly difficult, that price competition between academic institutions for limited funding will improve presentational skills but drive down more fundamental academic quality. However, in general it is usually possible for research sponsors to assess the quality of research groups they support, for example, by funding pilot projects before committing large sums of money.

More difficult to be optimistic about is the concern that much teaching and research with long-term value may be lost if higher education institutions have to show clear evidence of immediate value for money in all their activities. Much of the most worthwhile research and inspiring teaching is done by unworldly academics who are not at their best in a world of glossy prospectuses, public relations presentations and rigid adherence to detailed budgets. If market forces are to determine research funding it is in no-one's interest to sponsor long-term speculative research for two reasons. One is simply that the returns are so long-term and risky that it is very difficult for any individual enterprise to bear them, even if overall basic research is known to bring solid long term economic returns. The second is that no matter how strong the patent laws it is almost impossible to protect intellectual rights in fundamental discoveries for any significant period of time. This is the classic free-rider problem in economics. Many of the benefits from basic research accrue to those who had no stake in the original investment. Thus in the absence of public funding there will be a less than optimal amount of investment in basic research. One problem with this argument is that even governments need to take some account of the extent to which their own taxpayers will benefit from the outcomes of the research. It used to be a widely made criticism of British scientists and technologists that while they were good at obtaining Nobel prizes, few of their discoveries were turned into marketable products by British companies.

Funding and institutional management

There are contrasting models of the long-term effects of funding mechanisms on academic organizations. At one extreme is the view that organizations based on knowledge, cognition and communication have inherent structures determined by essential epistemological and psychological principles. Changes do occur. New subjects are taught, the basic units of academic organization evolve: but it happens in response to the internal dynamic of academic life: new research findings; new theories about the nature of teaching and learning; or simply interpersonal transactions within the institution. Academic activity may respond superficially to changing external pressures but its essential core is untouched. This is the model that underlies the analyses of academic organization and disciplines put forward by Clark (1984) Becher and Kogan (1980) and Becher (1989).

At the other extreme academic organization is seen as a social construct dependent as much on its external environment as on its own deep structures and value systems. Hague (1991), for example, among many others believes that ways of organizing knowledge and learning that have been successful in the past may not be appropriate for the economic and technological environment of the present and future.

One prediction of the first model is that while financial and administrative mechanisms antipathetic to underlying academic structures may restrict scholarly activity, it can camouflage itself or retreat into its inner shell and emerge unscathed when circumstances become more favourable. The chameleon may change its colour but the animal underneath remains the same. However, according to a more gloomy version of this thesis, if the climate is too hostile for too prolonged a period the chameleon will no longer be able to cope and will become extinct: 'the university in any meaningful sense of the word will cease to exist' (Wasser, 1990).

The second model predicts continuous adaptive responses to changing external circumstances but the genes remain the same and continuity is ensured. Academic activities change and may be organised differently but there is no reason to suppose that anything of value is lost unless it is replaced by something of greater worth in terms of an ever-shifting social and economic environment. This is the assumption which has underpinned government policy in Britain and several other countries during the 1980s.

Burgess, (1982) made a distinction between an 'autonomous tradition', 'aloof, academic, conservative and exclusive', and a 'service tradition', 'responsive, vocational, innovating and open'. He related the first model to

British universities and the second to polytechnics and colleges. In terms of this analysis there has been a considerable shift since 1981 towards the service tradition by both universities and non-university institutions, which in some respects, is paradoxical, since all polytechnics and major colleges are now autonomous. A likely explanation is that both universities and non-university institutions are now in a market environment, whereas Burgess was describing a situation in which it was taken for granted that higher education was heavily subsidized by government general grants.

The changing patterns of finance are seen by many academics as a threat, and there certainly are risks. However, they also offer opportunities. Well-managed institutions that are responsive to national needs can find resources from a variety of sources to carry out their fundamental academic functions of scholarship, social criticism and the creation of new knowledge. Many have done so in the 1980s and will continue to do so in the 1990s. The real challenge, for institutions as well as for national funding bodies in Britain, will be to retain the best features of the collegial and the bureaucratic models while responding positively to market opportunities.

During the period covered by this study, general grants to universities, with little detailed accountability for their use, were replaced by a system where virtually all funds received are deemed to be for specific services rendered. Polytechnics and colleges, which at the beginning of the 1980s, were for the most part subject to line-by-line budgets and administered according to local authority procedures, are now autonomous and funded for teaching in a way that is similar in all essentials to universities; and they have the imminent prospect of being called universities and funded as such.

Whether or not these changes will meet all the aspirations of their protagonists is not yet clear. However, this study has shown that the ways in which higher education institutions receive their funds do have a powerful influence on their internal resource allocation and management mechanisms and so affect incentives, organizational behaviour and the composition of the academic services that are provided.

Resource allocation mechanisms that are appropriate when funds for a range of activities are allocated to the institution as a whole, leaving it to decide within broad limits how they are to be allocated amongst individual operating groups, are not necessarily the most efficient when the institution is in effect earning income for each 'product' or 'service' separately. When most of an institution's income is general core funding, the main resource allocation decision is how to allocate income in accordance with academic priorities determined within the institution. Financial management is largely a matter of bookkeeping. In this model the central administration of the university or polytechnic may be seen as a monopolistic buyer of academic services from dependent departments and research centres. Central administration (which may of course be mediated by participatory decision making procedures) is in a position to regulate academic activity.

When, however, a large proportion of income is 'earned' from the sale of specific services financial management is in a sense reversed. There was a marked shift during the 1980s from administrative allocation and regulation to a more varied system of financial management, involving incentives, levies, management information and cost analysis. Financial management of higher education institutions now has four main tasks:

1. To encourage subsidiary units to generate income from teaching and research.
2. To appropriate at least part of the surpluses arising from this income for the provision of common services and the promotion of institutional priorities.
3. To ensure that short-run income maximization does not jeopardize long-run market position by allowing quality to deteriorate.
4. To ensure that all moneys are properly accounted for in accordance with legal and financial regulations.

In this model the departments are in effect *buying* management services from the centre and if these services are not cost-effective they may seek them, formally or informally, from elsewhere. The disintegration of London University as anything but a loose academic federation and central servicing unit is a very likely outcome of these pressures. Similar pressures are likely to be felt in other large institutions, particularly where there are powerful medical, engineering and business schools which have direct access to large amounts of external funds.

When institutions are autonomous and income comes from many sources in the form of payment for services rendered, they must respond to opportunities as they arise. Broad mission statements and corporate logos convey a marketing image, but these must be complemented by opportunistic policies and strategies that find and exploit niches in an ever-changing market place. The flexibility required for such responsiveness is sometimes shown by well-led centralized management structures able to marshal the resources of a whole institution quickly; but the need to provide easily perceived incentives for income generation has also led to devolution of routine financial responsibilities. There are some signs that polytechnics have been moving towards the more centralized management model whereas universities are more likely to be devolving financial and other management responsibilities to departments and faculties. There may be vestiges of the old autonomous versus service traditions at work. The universities preserve some elements of intellectual exclusiveness by devolving many marketing decisions to discipline-based departments, while polytechnics are more accustomed to interdisciplinary problem based teaching and research and centrally regulated responses to outside pressures. Some universities now resemble franchising operations in which the central authority imposes a levy on departmental franchisees in return for the provision of central services and a corporate image. There are, however, important exceptions on either side: several polytechnics have adopted the decentralized model following incorporation and some successful universities remain highly centralized.

The current orthodoxy in universities, deriving largely from the Jarratt Report (1985) is that devolution of financial responsibilities to departmental cost centres encourages awareness of the opportunity cost of resources and provides incentives for income generation. This is based on the assumption that the dominant loyalty of academics is to their subjects and disciplines and thence to specialized academic departments and centres, so academics exert themselves for the basic departmental unit more willingly than for the institution as a whole. This corresponds to Becher's view of academic disciplines as tribes whose members support each other against incursions from outsiders (Becher, 1989). The Jarratt model was an attempt to mediate such tribal conflicts within the institution by devolving detailed decisions to the lowest possible managerial unit while retaining strategic planning and resource allocation decisions at the centre.

An alternative approach used successfully in some polytechnics and a few medium-sized universities is to encourage corporate institutional loyalty that is as powerful as disciplinary loyalties. This is achieved through good internal systems of communication, close involvement of the central administration with all aspects of institutional affairs, ensuring that both departments and individuals are suitably rewarded for activities that further the interests of the whole institution and, in some notable cases, through charismatic institutional leadership. If such a strategy is successful it can enable a university or polytechnic to harness the whole of its resources more readily than unstable coalitions of separate departmental cost centres. There may, however, be limits to the size and diversity of an institution which can usefully follow this model. Whether staff engaged primarily on part time, essentially remedial, teaching of 'access' students can ever make common cause in any real sense with researchers on the fundamental problems of physics is very doubtful.

While the case for departmental autonomy – that it encourages awareness of opportunity costs; that departmental loyalty is likely to encourage individuals to work harder; and that comparisons of departmental performance help central administrators determine priorities – is powerful, there are also strong arguments pointing the other way. They are first that the smaller the cost centre the less likely it is that it will have staff who have the necessary expertise to take informed resource allocation decisions or the management information systems to enable them to do so; that time spent on management may be at the expense of primary academic work; and that departmental enthusiasm should not be allowed to replace loyalty to the institution as a whole. The force of most of these criticisms are very much reduced when financial devolution is accompanied by appropriate training and administrative back-up.

Two related issues are the optimal size of decision-making units and the number of subordinate units that one level of management can oversee, and more theoretically the nature of management in academic organizations.

On the first a widespread view is that executive heads ought not to have more than about 15 subordinate units reporting directly to them. Applying the same logic to the size of departments, no head of department should have to deal directly with more than about 15–20 academic staff. Thus any institution with more than about 300 academic staff, or, 4,000 students, would need to have some intermediate management structure between its central administration and the operating units.

The theoretical issue is not so clear cut. If it is to operate efficiently, any enterprise where the relationship between inputs and outputs is complex, and which depends on high level professional skills requires mechanisms for achieving consensus that are both broad and deep. The quality of the services provided must depend to a substantial extent on the professional integrity and sense of 'ownership' of the practitioners. This suggests that quite apart from technical issues of span of management control, a measure of devolution of responsibilities is essential. However, it is possible to separate academic and financial management. The traditional university division between Senate authority for academic affairs and Council responsibility for financial matters was one approach.

However, this sharp distinction was difficult to maintain when resource shortages meant that financial priorities impinged directly on specific details of academic activity, and even minor academic choices were severely constrained by financial considerations. Financial stringency means that academic decisions, even at the lowest level must take some account of their financial implications, and financial decisions have direct academic consequences. Devolution of financial responsibility forces the academic operating units to face up to the hard choices that have to be made: but it may equally be an abdication by senior managers of their responsibility for taking and implementing difficult decisions. Different solutions to these dilemmas are being adopted in different institutions, and in a competitive situation it will no doubt be those that show the most fitness for purpose which survive. Of the institutions visited during the course of the research for this study, it appears that medium-sized academic enterprises (that is between 5,000 and 10,000 conventional students), with a fairly homogeneous range of activities and effective central financial and academic management, were the more successful during the 1980s. There are not economies of scale in higher education as there are in the automobile industry for example, and large multifaceted institutions have not proved to be markedly successful, unless they are split into medium-sized self-managing units. On the other hand, in a competitive world where marketing and corporate image are significant it is difficult for very small scale activities to obtain the recognition that the quality of their activities may merit.

Pricing policies and related issues

In a market-orientated higher education system it is important that all funding agencies should pay the full costs of academic services they support and that this should include an appropriate surplus. Academic establishments in Britain have charitable status and they are non-profit seeking, but in many essential respects they are commercial enterprises. If they were fully commercial they would include in their costs an allowance for a financial return to their owners. The charitable foundations' equivalent of profits (out of which future investment is financed) is the activities which they consider important but which other sponsors do not wish to subsidize. If all funding is deemed to be contractual and supplied in return for the provision of specific academic services, it is essential that all contracts contain a component analogous to profits that can be used to fund activities of a university or polytechnic's own choosing, and so permit it to accumulate intellectual and physical capital for future developments.

Many finance officers believe that at present external funding brings little net income because services are underpriced. Some argue that this is why many academic institutions are in financial trouble despite staff claims about being overworked: all their products are underpriced. Most universities and polytechnics have begun to tackle this matter and to develop standard formulae for pricing externally funded activities and for allocating the proceeds between individuals, cost centres and central services.

It is important to distinguish between *costs* and *prices*. Prices have to be fixed on the basis of what the market will bear. The purpose of detailed costing is to determine whether what the market will bear is financially worthwhile. A critical issue is to determine which supporting activities should be included in indirect costs. Pricing policies are, however, complicated because in addition to income generation, academic institutions may undertake some external research, teaching and consultancy because they enable members of staff to do work of intrinsic academic value; or they may serve the function of promotional advertising, establishing contacts that will produce students or larger research contracts in the future; or they may be seen as personal development, providing opportunities for staff, and students, to broaden their work experiences.

Attempts to institute realistic costing and pricing of income-generating activities are creating tensions, sometimes severe, between departmental staff and central administrators. Many academic staff claim the right to do a particular piece of research or teaching primarily because it is academically or socially worthwhile, but the finance office must be concerned with the question of how the full long-run costs of an institution's whole portfolio of activities are to be covered. When substantial indirect costs *are* recovered, academics in the departments which have earned them often resent the overheads going to what they see as the central administration or other less active departments. This is resulting in powerful fissiparous tendencies in some institutions. There are already cases where income-generating activities have split away from their parent institutions and incentives for unilateral declarations of independence are likely to increase.

Thus a fundamental question for all academics and institutional managers is the rationale for undertaking any income generating work that is not directly related to the central academic mission. One view is that a higher education institution exists to teach undergraduate and postgraduate students and, in the case of universities at least, to pursue scholarship and basic research, and that these should be paid for out of public funds. At the opposite extreme is the view that higher education institutions are economic enterprises in the knowledge industry, and they have the right to determine their portfolio of activities on cost-effectiveness and efficiency criteria alone. When publicly-funded conventional undergraduate and postgraduate courses were the most profitable range of services any conflict was largely theoretical and could be left to the philosophers of higher education. When, however, core public funding is inadequate for a university or polytechnic to be viable if it depends on what it can earn from these activities it must shrink or it must diversify. The function of external income is to help maintain the economic viability and hence the academic integrity of the institution. But under the purist academic model it can do this only if *surpluses* are generated, while under what may be called the relativist market model any legitimate activity the institution undertakes is as valuable as any other provided it earns its keep.

A specific issue is the staffing of income generating activities. Most polytechnics and universities have established, or are in the process of establishing, institutional consultancy services which aim to be surplus generating. In many there are tensions between staff of the self-financing units, and established staff and managers of the parent institution. Conditions of work of contract staff are frequently poor and their job security minimal. Relatively haphazard arrangements for the employment of non-established staff have been acceptable in the past because they were a relatively small proportion of total academic staff employed, many of the jobs were seen as apprenticeships for permanent employment, and until the late 1980s generally depressed employment prospects for graduates meant that some highly qualified recruits were available even with these unfavourable working conditions. This has changed in several subject areas. It is proving extremely difficult to recruit staff under these employment conditions in such areas as computing, engineering and business studies. Demographic trends make it probable, despite the severe recession of the early 1990s, that the recruitment of able graduates in subject areas where they are most needed will become more difficult in the 1990s. One of the most urgent problems facing the management of higher education institutions is to devise employment and conditions of service that reduce the gaps between permanent academic staff and those employed on specific contract work. In general the employment conditions of academics is likely to be a major management issue of the 1990s as institutions diversify their activities and become more financially independent.

There is widespread concern about the amount of administrative and academic time spent in bidding for funds and accounting for their use, though as Chapter 8 has shown, in most cases the opportunity costs of bidding for specific grants during the 1980s does not appear to have been exorbitant. A particular concern is that development funds are rarely available to enable bids to be prepared, and in many cases even successful bidders are not allowed to offset the cost of preparing the bid against the income received. In the past UGC and NAB core funding effectively financed the cost of bidding for other initiatives. Whether this will continue to be possible under UFC and PCFC contracts and marginal cost funding of students is very doubtful and this is one of the reasons for the difficult cash flow position of several universities and polytechnics.

There is also some concern that the deadlines for many funding initiatives make it impossible to process bids through what were previously considered to be normal academic consultative channels. To this extent, the expansion of earmarked funding may have saved academic time by reinforcing trends towards more hierarchical and less participatory management systems, though whether this is at the expense of the unquantifiable benefits of collegiality is an open question.

Funding choices

This study has shown that in many respects higher education institutions are behaving as multi-product firms in which the portfolio of activities is determined by the changing cost of inputs and the changing market conditions for each of its product ranges. The production function is complex; some activities are complementary with each other and some competitive. Most are partly complementary and partly competitive. Changes in amounts and patterns of funding change both the balance between academic and supporting activities and the composition of academic activities. The former is showing itself mainly in the amount of academic staff time devoted to seeking funds, managing them and accounting formally for their use. The changes in the composition of academic activity are primarily the substantial increase in contract research and a shift of emphasis away from students on traditional integrated award-bearing courses towards different kinds of students on courses that are modular and those that are not award-bearing in the traditional academic sense. There has also been a big increase in the number of older students and of students without traditional entry qualifications. The distribution by subject area has changed with big increases in business related courses and reductions in many arts related subjects and in physical sciences. There is increased separation of research and teaching.

Higher education is concerned with long-term and frequently intangible benefits. There are intrinsic disagreements about objectives and about the best ways of achieving agreed objectives. In both their teaching and research roles, academic institutions have the responsibility, and should have the means, to stand aloof from the whims of current fashion, and to be concerned with underlying realities. But at the same time they cannot ignore entirely what is happening in the world outside their walls. These tensions can be made creative rather than destructive with appropriate financial management. Many different sources of funding and many different criteria for the disbursement of funds may complicate the lives of academic chief executives and their administrative support staff, but they are one way of ensuring the capacity of higher education institutions to perform their wide variety of legitimate roles, including research for its own sake that may or may not bring long-term benefits, the maintenance of a cultural heritage and the preservation of long-term intellectual values.

A mass higher education system must be a differentiated system. Indeed, there are legitimate doubts about whether the term 'higher education' any longer has real meaning covering, as it does, activities that range from research and scholarship at the very frontiers of knowledge to near remedial access courses and short periods of adult retraining. It is not realistic to expect single institutions, however large, to perform this whole range of activities equally efficiently. A considerable degree of institutional specialization is necessary. There are essentially two ways of achieving institutional differentiation: one is to allocate functions through strategic planning; the other is for the distinctive features of each institution to evolve through the operation of market forces. At present British higher education is set to go down the latter path with both main funding agencies, as well as most of the subsidiary funders encouraging market competition. Furthermore, as this study has shown, many universities and polytechnics are using market indicators of performance as a basis for their internal resource allocation.

The question arises of whether the interplay of market pressures brings about optimal, or satisfactory, long-run allocation of resources to and within higher education. There are four questions:

1. Will response to market indicators bring about an optimal or satisfactory total expenditure on higher education?
2. Will the resources be used effectively and efficiently within institutions?
3. Is the pattern of resource allocation brought about by the market socially acceptable in other ways?
4. If the market is providing less than perfect answers is this a case for moving towards a planning approach or for intervening in the market to remove imperfections?

The answers suggested by this study, which has examined the issue from the viewpoint of higher education institutions, is that the market does work but not perfectly. Some institutions have taken much longer than others to come to terms with market forces. There are problems about cutting corners on quality which are beginning to be tackled, but the experience of full cost fees for overseas students is not wholly encouraging in this respect. External intervention, in the arrangements for quality assurance are justified. There is also a case, at a time when most of the pressures are for formal standardization of higher education institutions, enabling them all to compete on equal terms in all parts of this very heterogeneous market, for some external designation of primary function. It is possibly true that in the long run the interplay of market forces will bring about satisfactory differentiation of institutional functions, but it is likely to take several years before a university accepts, for example, that the contributions it can make to basic research are strictly limited. The period of adjustment would be more protracted if funds for research were allocated on the basis of competitive bidding with price being a major determinant of success.

The needs of research are very different from those of teaching in a mass higher education system. One result of a variety of purposes and criteria in teaching institutions is that research cannot perform the same function in all of them. Much scientific research requires expensive scientific equipment and there are undoubted benefits from a concentration of effort. Moreover, there are few direct links between undergraduate teaching and many areas of research. Until the mid-1980s it was generally claimed, at least in universities, that teaching and research were complementary and inextricably linked. However, in recent years, since selective funding of research was introduced by the UGC, the distinctiveness of the two functions and the possible conflicts between them have received more attention. There is a growing realization that not all students benefit from close association with research scientists. For many it is advantageous to have the opportunity of working alongside industrial, commercial and professional practitioners and to be taught by expert communicators and popularizers rather than research workers with continuous first-hand experience. For researchers regular teaching commitments may be a distraction. As science becomes more and more specialized, the knowledge gap between scientists at the frontiers of knowledge and the majority of students increases. While the individual university teacher, working alone or with a small team can continue to make advances in some areas, it is increasingly the case that modern equipment and frequent rapid communication between scientists is the prime need for major scientific progress. This increases the comparative advantage of specialized research groups.

A role for the Higher Education Funding Council

In July 1991 the PCFC and the UFC received new instructions from the Secretary of State for Education and Science in preparation for merger:

> The government wishes to see the public funds available to higher education spent in such a way as to secure cost-effective and efficient expansion. The allocation of funds by the Funding Councils will need to complement the effects of public funds available to each institution

through tuition fees. I see the following key principles as continuing to inform the distribution of funds for teaching and research:

(a) there should be a means of specifying clearly what it is that institutions are expected to provide in return for public funds; funding should be seen to reward both quality and efficiency;

(b) means need to be in place for assessing quality in both teaching and research;

(c) there will need to be arrangements for measuring and rewarding institutional efficiency;

(d) the allocations should have regard to the distinct missions of individual institutions and to the need to ensure that the best features are both maintained and built upon. Such missions might evolve over time, but the funding methodology should not attempt abrupt change, or development into areas where the institution concerned had no natural advantage; and

(e) the resulting selectivity and allocations should be tempered by regard to academic and financial viability. In particular, allocations should not lead to year to year changes in income greater than institutions can reasonably be required to accommodate.

This makes it clear that while the government still envisages student demand as having a prime role in determining the pattern of higher education development it will be the role of the new funding council to moderate that pattern to take account of quality and efficiency issues that are not dealt with satisfactorily by market forces.

The new HEFC will have to form a view on four main issues.

1. To what extent should it seek to reinforce market forces and to what extent is its role one of intervention by a large, but minority funder to correct the excesses of the market, much as the Bank of England and the Bundesbank intervene to regulate money markets? In particular how is it to interpret requirement (c) above in the case of an institution which runs into serious financial difficulty because it fails to recruit enough students?

2. How will it interpret its function with respect to issues of equity, efficiency and quality? Should its main concern be to spread its resources widely in order to provide access to some form of higher education for as many students as possible? Or should it concentrate at least part of its funds on a smaller number of relatively expensive institutions on the grounds that even a mass higher education system must have some élite elements? In particular should it continue to have a significant role in the funding of research?

3. What should be its role in promoting innovation? Will it have a role in stimulating quality improvement apart from rewarding it after the event?

4. While recognizing that it has clearly a function of protecting the

integrity of existing higher education institutions should its main focus be on funding institutions or on activities within institutions?

The final ending of the binary line and with it the last vestiges of the assumptions which governed higher education policy in the post Robbins period make it a particularly opportune time to undertake a fundamental review of the role of public funding mechanisms. Between the Second World War and 1980 the state effectively accepted the responsibility of providing higher education as a public service and this position was legitimated by the Robbins Committee and the government policies which followed it. Although in principle the universities received a deficiency grant, in practice UGC grants were an almost unconditional subsidy from government which covered three-quarters of their expenditure: other government subsidies accounted for most of the rest. Non-university institutions were funded explicitly as public service institutions. With this dominant funding role came a planning function that involved the establishment of priorities and selective resource allocation in accordance with these priorities. Institutional resource allocation arrangements adjusted to these dominant funding models. When the system was expanding rapidly selectivity concentrated on capital expenditure: when there was little growth this was ineffective and selectivity had to be in relation to recurrent funding. This was at the heart of much of the tension between higher education institutions and their funding agencies during the 1980s.

Now the role of core public funding agencies is very much reduced in terms of their percentage contribution to total recurrent expenditure. It is likely that when the new HEFC is established it will provide less than 40 per cent of the income of higher education institutions. It is sometimes claimed that the Funding Councils exist at all only because the Treasury feels able to cash limit funds available to funding bodies in a way that it believes would be much more difficult if the market were simulated by means of vouchers to students. Apart from this overall cash limit the UFC and PCFC were encouraged to be almost completely passive in the establishment of priorities, and to respond to bids from institutions which are themselves expected to respond to student pressures. However, as the July 1991 letter shows there are signs that the government has changed its position on this issue. It is paradoxical but true that in a system where there is little growth of resources and little capital expenditure, a funding council that provides only a small part of the recurrent funding of higher education institutions is in a more powerful position to establish priorities than one that provides over three-quarters of their resources. It can no longer be expected to be responsible for the overall health of the whole system and the survival of individual institutions within it. Rather it can use its resources to promote developments that the market is unable to ensure. Chapter 8 has shown how relatively small amounts of expenditure can exert powerful leverage on the system if they are strategically used and sharply focused. Quality improvement, broader access, encouragement of inter-institutional collaboration, teaching innovations to take advantage of new technology, and basic research infrastructure are five areas where there are grounds for doubting whether market forces will by themselves ensure an optimal allocation of resources and where relatively small contributions from the funding councils could have a disproportionate effect.

If the new Funding Councils do see themselves as having a more proactive role than their immediate predecessors there are several models in other OECD countries that merit examination. In the USA, for example, the public sector ensures basic higher education provision at low cost for all comers (obviously in a country as large and as heterogeneous as the USA there are differences of detail between states), while individuals who want education with particular characteristics buy places in private universities and colleges which receive little institutional support from public funds. This contrasts with Japan where the great national universities are explicitly meritocratic and set standards by which the much larger number of private universities can be judged by their clients. In British terms the difference can be expressed in terms of alternative ways in which the Funding Councils might behave. Under the USA model public funding would be reduced in universities such as Oxford and Cambridge, on the grounds that they offer special advantages to private individuals that could not possibly be replicated across the rest of the system: under the Japanese model these universities and perhaps a few others would receive especially favourable treatment and would set national standards by which the performance of other institutions could be assessed.

Another model is that currently in operation in France and Australia, where individual contracts are agreed with whole institutions for the provision of an agreed range of academic services over a period of several years. If it were felt that there is a real danger of institutional fragmentation, as has been suggested in this study, that would be one way of strengthening central institutional managements as well as ensuring identifiable and distinct missions for each institution.

Alternatively the Council could examine some of the formula funding techniques that have been developed in Denmark and the Netherlands and use part of its resources to fund graduates rather than student numbers. This might help to ensure that increased access results in an increased output of persons with useful qualifications and not merely increased numbers of students failing to complete their courses satisfactorily.

To set out these models is not to advocate them, but it does highlight the need for further clarification of the function of public funding in higher education subsidy in relation to specified national aims. If increased access and market simulation were the sole aim, vouchers for students provide a more effective mechanism than institutional bidding from a bureaucratic funding agency.

It is misleading to claim that market forces are now the only influence on British higher education. However, there have been perceptible shifts in this direction during the 1980s, and forthcoming substantial increases in fees and the transfer of further funds from the UFC to the research councils are further steps in this direction. They are seen in many universities and some polytechnics and colleges as threats and they will certainly stimulate further changes in their organizational behaviour and academic portfolios.

Charges of complacency and inertia in higher education institutions had some validity in the 1960s and 1970s; though it is a legitimate defence that it was complacency caused by high student demand for their services. In the 1980s the reaction against complacency may have resulted in too much attention being paid to short-term, easily identifiable economic and social returns and not enough to the longer term intangible social and cultural outcomes of teaching, research and scholarship. Higher education institutions need to have some space to stand apart from society's changing fashions as well as to respond constructively to them. The encouragement of a certain degree of academic distance from the market to help meet the claims of quality and equality and other national priorities is the proper role of a core funding council in a period when the greater part of university and polytechnic income is likely to continue to be market led.

Appendix: Research Methodology

Twenty-four institutions of higher education were visited for 2 or more days during the period January to April 1989. They included 14 universities, eight polytechnics and two other PCFC colleges. The selection of universities was based primarily on an analysis of Form 3 returns, as published by the University Statistical Record. Each university was allocated to one of four approximately equal size groups, which were defined on the basis of their financial experiences since 1980. Group 1 were those universities which had received above average treatment by the UGC between 1980 and 1987 and had also increased their non-UGC income by an above average amount. Group 2 were those that have been favourably treated by the UGC but which have had less than average success in raising their non-UGC income. Group 3 were those which had below average treatment by the UGC but has compensated to some extent by an above average performance in increasing external earnings. Group 4 were those that received below-average treatment by the UGC and had less than average success in increasing external earnings. There are some problems with this method of classification in that a university that already had a high level of external income in 1980 might have more difficulty in increasing this than one which had very little external income. However, since the emphasis of this study is on changing financial arrangements it seemed more important to try to identify factors associated with changing patterns of income rather than merely to describe the historical situation of particular universities. Subsequently, universities were selected from each of the groups to ensure that there was a reasonable geographic distribution (including Scotland and Wales) and a reasonable spread between the main types of universities (former colleges of advanced technology, universities established in the 1960s, civic universities and Oxbridge). Of the 14 universities initially selected, two declined to take part and were replaced by two others as similar as possible on the above criteria.

Less detailed information was available for the non-university institutions. In the case of the polytechnics, an attempt was made to select some which had benefited and some which had suffered from NAB/formula funding and some were chosen with high external earnings and some where these were apparently low. Again efforts were made to secure a reasonable geographical spread. In the case of the colleges two institutions of contrasting types were selected on a random basis. Of the eight polytechnics selected initially, one was unable to take part and was replaced by another with similar characteristics. Three other institutions of higher education were initially selected mainly on the basis of suggestions made by members of the project Steering Committee. The three were intended to reflect some of the variety of different types of institutions in this group. One declined to take part at quite a late stage and was not replaced. In summary, therefore, the study reflects the position in a wide cross-section of universities and polytechnics at the end of the 1980s and any remarks about other institutions must be considered as indicative only.

The study relies heavily, though far from exclusively, on evidence from the case study institutions. This evidence was of two types. One was documentary evidence of income and expenditure of the institution and any associated trusts and companies, organizational structure, management information systems, resource allocation formulae and bids for funds in the past few years. The other source of information was semi-structured interviews with senior academics and administrators. These covered four kinds of evidence. The first was factual material not readily available in documentary form, for example reasons for organizational changes. The second was interpretation of documentary evidence such as the relationship between university or polytechnic companies and the parent institutions. The third qualitative assessment of the effects on the institutions of specific changes in funding. Finally more speculative views were sought about future developments and their likely effects.

The interviews were based on the list of questions and topics for discussion shown in Annex I. Their length varied from half an hour to two and a half hours. At each stage the interviewees were asked to support their statements with documentary evidence wherever possible. The report on each interview was sent back to the interviewee for verification. The analysis of documentary evidence and the verified interview reports formed the basis of 24 institutional case studies which it was agreed with the respondents should remain anonymous.

All the universities, polytechnics and colleges which took part made detailed arrangements for members of the research team to meet senior members of administrative and academic staff. Many answered probing questions and made available much documentary material. All this was at a time of extremely heavy administrative and academic workload, particularly in the polytechnics and colleges sector. More than the usual expressions of gratitude are due to all the individuals who took part, particularly those in each institution who made the arrangements for the visits. In all 243 individuals were interviewed. Table A.1 classifies them according to their main functions.

In broad terms, the period of change with which this study is concerned is the 1980s. Convenient base lines were the 'July 1981 cuts' in the case of the universities and the establishment of the NAB. However, in general the cuts of the early 1980s were seen as water under the bridge, and most of the senior academics and administrators interviewed were more concerned with the changes in the philosophy of funding that has been occurring since the middle of the 1980s.

None of the PCFC institutions was able to provide figures of total external income with any degree of confidence. Financial administration of the main budgets by local authorities inhibited the development of the concept of the polytechnic as a single economic enterprise. Grant and contract income was usually recorded in separate memorandum accounts and often the aggregates were not assembled for the whole institution.

The two non-polytechnic PCFC institutions in the sample differed widely. One was a small monotechnic and the other a large college, not dissimilar in its range of activities from a polytechnic.

All universities reported that they had applied for funds under most UGC and

Table A.1   Categories of persons interviewed in case-study institutions

Heads of institutions	10
Deputy and assistant heads of institutions	27
Members of finance offices	35
Planning officers	5
Registrars	18
Continuing education specialists	22
Industrial liaison specialists	18
Overseas student specialists	7
External relations specialists	8
Heads of university and polytechnic companies	9
Heads of self-financing units and centres	8
Other administration	13
Members of science departments	21
Members of technology departments	18
Members of other academic departments	24
Total	243

Some individuals were interviewed in more than one capacity. Where this occurred they have been attributed to the highest category in the above list.

research council initiatives, sometimes on the grounds that not to do so would imply a lack of interest in that area. Of the 14 visited, 11 had made bids for Alvey funds; 11 bid for Engineering and Technology Programme funds; 12 made one or more bids for an Interdisciplinary Research Centre; 13 bid for funds under the PICKUP Programme and 10 bid for the Enterprise in Higher Education Programme during its first year. Amongst the eight polytechnics all had bid for ETP and EHE funds, three for Alvey funds and two for IRCs.

Annex I: Interview Schedule

Topic One: General Trends during the 1980s

To be asked of head of institution *plus* 1 or 2 other people concerned with its central direction.

Question
What do you consider to be the most significant changes in the sources of funds for this institution since 1981(2)?

Question
How have these changes affected the academic and administrative activities of the university/polytechnic?

Question
How have management systems and styles been affected?

Question
Which activities (Departments, Centres, Research Units) in the institution have proved to be particularly successful in attracting outside funds?

Question
What are your most successful examples of liaison between industry or commerce and the university/polytechnic?

Topic Two: Future Prospects and Attitudes to Them

Question
What do you consider to be the most likely changes in the future funding arrangements for your institution and how do you think you are likely to be affected by them?

MSC (Training Agency) Enterprise Initiative bid (whether or not successful)
Interdisciplinary research centre bid (whether or not successful)
Alvey programme
Engineering/Technology programme (the Switch)
Overseas students active recruitment
Continuing education [in particular: PICKUP, GRIST/LEATGS, Short (non-award bearing) full-cost courses]

Teaching company schemes (SERC)
Industrial liaison in general
Any significant projects involving industrial or commercial funding that are not
    included above

Questions for financial secretary or equivalent.

Topic Three: Contracts and Quasi-contracts

Question
*What proportion of the income of this university/polytechnic is in the form of payment for
specific services?*

Question
How do you determine the cost at which such services are made available?

Question
*Can you briefly describe any limited companies or other self financing units associated with the
university/polytechnic?*

Question
*How much in total has this university/polytechnic earned from industry and commerce during
the past year and how does this compare with the figure five years ago?*

Topic Four: Arrangements for Internal Resource Allocation

Question
*How have your internal resource allocation arrangements been affected by the changes in
UGC/NAB procedures?*

Question
*How has the expansion of non-UGC/NAB funding affected internal resource allocation
arrangements?*

Question
What are the institution's policy and practice with respect to overhead charges?

Question
*How much Indemnity Insurance does the Institution have against claims resulting from its
commercial activities?*

Topic Five: Staffing Issues

Questions probably best put to secretary or registrar in university, deputy director
responsible for academic staff in polytechnics.

Question
What are the main changes in staffing that have resulted from the funding changes?

Question
*What are the main obstacles to academic staff responsiveness to external financial
opportunities?*

Topic Six: Training Agency Enterprise Initiative

Questions for person(s) responsible for submitting institutional bid (whether or not successful)

Question
How much staff time, if possible costed in some way, went into submitting the bid?

Question
Please summarize the proposal you made.

Question
Description of present state of programme.

Question
Are the contractual arrangements with the Training Agency in any way an infringement on the autonomy of the university/polytechnic?

Topic Seven: Interdisciplinary Research Centres

Questions for person(s) responsible for submitting institutional bid (whether or not successful)

Question
How much staff time, if possible costed in some way, went into submitting the bid?

Question
Please summarize the proposal you made.

Question to successful bidders only
What have been the benefits so far of the creation of the IRC?

Question
What have been the main problems in establishing the IRC?

Topic Eight: The Alvey Programme

Questions for person(s) responsible for submitting institutional bid (whether or not successful)

Question
How much staff time, if possible costed in some way, went into submitting any bids?

Question
Please summarize the proposal you made.

Question
What has been achieved under the programme?

Question
What effect has Alvey funding had on research and other academic work in the institution generally?

Question
Can you give us names of the companies they collaborate with?

Topic Nine: Engineering/Technology Programme

Questions for person(s) responsible for submitting institutional bids (whether or not successful)

Question
How much staff time, if possible costed in some way, went into submitting any bids?

Question
Please summarize the proposals you made.

For successful bids only.

Question
What arrangements were made to allocate the funds received under the ETP?

Question
Has the scheme had any impact on the institution other than that resulting from the allocation of extra students to the departments directly concerned?

Topic Ten: Overseas Students

Remember that the main concern here, as in all the themes is with funding and its implications.

Question
What have been the main features of this institution's policy towards the recruitment of overseas students since the introduction of the full cost fees policy in 1980?

Question
What changes in courses and welfare arrangements have been made to take account of the special needs of overseas students?

Question
Has any system of internal rewards or incentives been established to take account of extra efforts at departmental level in recruiting and teaching students from overseas?

Question
May we have details of any contractual arrangements with the British Council, overseas governments or other agencies to ensure a regular supply of students on particular courses?

Question
How do you see overseas student numbers developing in the future at this institution?

Topic Eleven: Continuing Education Especially In-service Training of Teachers, 'PICKUP' and Customised Short Courses

Question
How has this university/polytechnic been affected by the changes in the funding arrangements for the in-service training of teachers in recent years?

Question
Has the university/polytechnic received any special funding from the UGC/NAB for new INSET work?

Question
What has been the institution's experience of the PICKUP programme?

Question
What other categories of short courses does the university/polytechnic offer and how successful are they?

Topic Twelve: Industrial and Commercial Links

Questions for Industrial Liaison Officer or similar person.

Question
Can we have a brief account of the main features of the development of industrial liaison in this university/polytechnic?

Question
What benefits other than income does the university/polytechnic obtain from industrial liaison?

Question
What have been the effects of the growth of business involvement on the academic activities of this university/polytechnic?

Topic Thirteen: Other Industrial Links

Questions for all individuals responsible for any major industrial/commercial link – teaching, research, consultancy.

Question
Please can you describe in detail the nature of the industrial link for which you are responsible?

Bibliography

Advisory Board for the Research Councils (ABRC) (1983). *The Support Given by Research Councils for In-house and University Research.* Working party report to the ABRC. London, ABRC.

ABRC (1987). *A Strategy for the Science Base.* London, ABRC.

ABRC (1988). *Science and Public Expenditure 1988: a Report to the Secretary of State for Education and Science.* London, ABRC.

Acherman, J. A. and Brons, R. (eds) (1989). *Changing Financial Relations between Government and Higher Education.* Uitgeverij Lemma, B. V. Culemborg.

Ashworth, J. M. (1983). 'Reshaping higher education in Britain', *Higher Education Review*, **15**(2), 59–67.

Ashworth, J. M. (1985). 'What price an ivory tower? University–industry relationships', *Higher Education Review*, **17**(2), 31–43.

Alewell, H. C. K. (1990). 'Financing universities in the Federal Republic of Germany', *Higher Education Quarterly*, **44**(2), 123–41.

Allison, L. (1990). 'Academic tenure and Conservative philosophy', *Higher Education Quarterly*, **44**(1), 35–59.

Altbach, P. G. (1984). 'The management of decline: An international perspective', *Higher Education in Europe*, **9**(4), 58–64.

Baker, K. (1989). *Science Policy: The Way Ahead. Speech to Academia.* London, HMSO.

Ball, R. (1986). *Strategic Planning in British Universities.* Paper presented at the 26th Annual Forum of the Association for Institutional Research. Orlando, FL, June 22–25.

Barnes, A. D. (1989). 'Technology transfer: A European perspective', *Industry and Higher Education*, March.

Barnes, J. and Barr, N. (1988). *Strategies for Higher Education: The Alternative White Paper.* Aberdeen, Aberdeen University Press.

Becher, T. and Kogan, M. (1980). *Process and Structure in Higher Education.* London, Heinemann. (2nd edn, Routledge, 1991.)

Becher, T. (1987). *British Higher Education.* London, Allen and Unwin.

Becher, T. (1989). *Academic Tribes and Territories.* Milton Keynes, Open University Press.

Beloff, Lord (1990). 'Universities and the public purse', *Higher Education Quarterly*, **44**(1), 3–20.

Berdahl, R. O. (1982). 'Great Britain – Cutting the budget, resetting the priorities', *Change*, **14**(5), 38–43.

Birch, D. W. *et al.* (1977). 'A note on costing the teaching activity in higher education', *College and University*, **6**(1), 67–74.

Bland, D. E. (1990). *Managing Higher Education*. London, Cassell.

Boorman, D. W. (1982). 'Better for less – British universities face the 80s', *Planning for Higher Education*, **11**(1), 30–34.

Bosworth, S. (1984). 'The management of staffing reductions in a time of acute financial crisis: The survival of a university', *International Journal of Institutional Management in Higher Education*, **8**(1), 49–66.

Bottomley, A. and Dunworth, J. (1972). *Rates of Return on University Education with Economies of Scale*. Bradford, Bradford University.

Bottomley, J. A. *et al.* (1972). *Costs and Potential Economie*. Paris, OECD.

Bourner, T. (1979). 'The "cost" of completing a part-time degree by full-time study', *Higher Education Review*, **12**(1), 55–69.

Brons, R. (1990). 'An investigation into the structure of higher education funding', *Higher Education Quarterly*, **44**(2), 142–54.

Bryant, R. J. (1984). 'Funding the universities and the 1982–84 triennium – Where did the money get to?', *Vestes*, **27**(2), 46–54.

Burgess, T. (1982). 'Autonomous and service traditions'. In Wagner, L. (ed.) *Agenda for Institutional Change in Higher Education*. Leverhulme Programme of Study into the Future of Higher Education, 3. Research into Higher Education Monographs, 45. London, SRHE.

Cannon, T. H. (1986). 'Research – A U.K. perspective', *Canadian Library Journal*, **43**(5), 281–4.

Clark, B. R. (1983). *The Higher Education System: Academic Organisation in Cross National Perspective*. Berkeley, University of California Press.

Clark, B. R. (1984). *Perspectives on Higher Education*. Berkeley, University of California Press.

Clayton, K. M. (1983). '"Buffer" institutions in higher education in the United Kingdom', *International Journal of Institutional Management in Higher Education*, **7**(2), 173–83.

Coldstream, P. (1989). 'Matching as matching', *Higher Education Quarterly*, **43**(2), 99–107.

Conference of University Administrators (CUA) (1976). *Proceedings of the Conference of University Administrators*. Newcastle, April. Manchester, CUA.

Conference of University Administrators (1984). *The Report of the CUA Working Party on Supplementary Sources of Funding for Universities in Great Britain*. Manchester, CUA.

Connor, A. I. *et al.* (1986). 'Academic–industry liaison in the United Kingdom: Economic perspectives', *Higher Education*, **15**(5), 407–20.

Craven, B. M. *et al.* (1983). 'Resource reallocation in higher education in Britain', *Higher Education*, **12**(5), 579–89.

Croham, Lord (1987). *A Review of the University Grants Committee*, Cmnd 81. London, HMSO.

CVCP (1988). *The Costing of Research Projects in Universities: A Report and Guidance to Universities*. London, CVCP.

Dennison, J. D. (1989). 'Higher education policy in the United Kingdom – Reformation or dissolution', *Canadian Journal of Higher Education*, **19**(1), 87–96.

DES (1973). *A Framework for Government Research and Development*, Cmnd 4814. London, HMSO.

DES (1978). *Higher Education into the 1990s. A Discussion Document*. London, DES; Edinburgh, Scottish Education Department.

DES (1985). *The Development of Higher Education into the 1990s*, Cmnd 9524. London, HMSO.

DES (1987). *Higher Education: Meeting the Challenge*. London, HMSO.

DES (1989). *Shifting the Balance of Public Funding of Higher Education to Fees: A Consultation Paper*. London, DES.

DES (1991). *Higher Education: A New Framework*. London, HMSO.

Dickson, D. (1982). 'British universities in turmoil', *Science*, **217**, 811–13.

Dolton, P. J. and Makepeace, G. H. (1982). 'University typology: A contemporary analysis', *Higher Education Review*, **14**(3), 33–47.

Dolton, P. J. and Makepeace, G. H. (1983). 'New blood or bad blood? The allocation of blood posts in British universities', *Higher Education Review*, **16**(1), 49–58.

Duncan, J. G. (1989). 'Marketing of higher education: Problems and issues in theory and practice', *Higher Education Quarterly*, **43**(2), 175–88.

Eustace, R. (1982). 'British higher education and the state', *European Journal of Education*, **17**(3), 283–94.

Farnham, D. (1985). 'Staffing in higher education: The emerging agenda', *Higher Education Review*, **18**(1), 43–60.

Flemming, J. (1989). *Review of the Interdisciplinary Research Centres: Report to the ABRC*.

Geddes, M. D. and Davies, A. J. I. (1983). 'The management of resources at Cranfield Institute of Technology', *International Journal of Institutional Management in Higher Education*, **7**(3), 261–71.

Gibbons, M. (1981). 'Universities and research: Response and challenge', *Higher Education Review*, **13**(3), 27–44.

Gordon, A. *et al.* (1984). 'Employer sponsorship of engineering students', *Research in Science and Technological Education*, **2**(2), 197–201.

Gupta, D. (1990). 'The Dawkins higher education plan: Its rationale and implications', *Higher Education Quarterly*, **44**(2), 154–62.

Guy, K. *et al.* (1991). *Evaluation of the Alvey Programme for Advanced Information Technology*. London, HMSO.

Hague, D. (1991). *Beyond Universities: A New Republic of the Intellect*. London, Institute of Economic Affairs.

Higgins, M. A. (1991). 'The student market', *Higher Education Quarterly*, **45**(1), 14–24.

Hirsh, W. and Morgan, R. (1978). 'Career prospects in British universities', *Higher Education*, **7**(1), 47–66.

HMSO (1963). *Higher Education Report of the Committee Appointed by the Prime Minister under the Chairmanship of Lord Robbins, 1961/63*. London, HMSO.

HMSO (Annual). *The Government Expenditure Plans*. London, HMSO.

Hopkins, D. S. P. and Massy, W. F. (1977). 'Long-range budget planning in private colleges and universities', *New Directions for Institutional Research*, **13**, 43–66.

Howarth, A. (1991). 'Market forces in higher education', *Higher Education Quarterly*, **45**(1), 5–13.

Hoy, J. C. and Bernstein, M. H. (eds) (1982). *Financing Higher Education: The Public Investment*. Boston, Auburn House Publishing Company.

Hutchinson, E. (1975). 'The origins of the University Grants Committee', *Minerva*, **13**(4), 583–620.

Jackson, C. (1981). 'Education cuts – Economic consequences', *Forum for the Discussion of New Trends in Education*, **23**(3), 60–63.

Jackson, R. (1989). 'Government and universities', *CRE-Action*, **89**(4), 69–76.

Jarratt, A. (1985). *Report of the Steering Committee on Efficiency Studies in Universities*. London, CVCP.

Jones, S. (1984). 'Reflections on a capped pool', *Higher Education Review*, **17**(1), 5–18.

Kerr, E. *et al.* (eds) (1987). *W(h)ither Binary? A Seminar on the Organisation of Higher Education for the 21st Century*. Report of Western Australian Post Secondary Education Commission, March. Nedlands.

Knight, P. (1981). 'The 1980–81 AFE pool: The end of an era', *Higher Education Review*, **14**(1), 17–31; **14**(3).

Knight, P. (1984). 'The 1984–85 NAB planning exercise: How great a failure?' *Higher Education Review*, **17**(1), 19–28.

Lancaster, D. *et al.* (1983). 'Operational research and its application in education management', *Educational Management and Administration*, **11**(3), 193–204.

Levy, J. C. (1987). 'Are research funds to engineering schools of real benefit to industry? A British viewpoint', *Engineering Education*, **77**(6), 324–8.

Leyland, D. G. (1986). 'Commercialism and corporate strategy in British higher education', *Higher Education Review*, **19**(1), 23–33.

Lieven, M. (1989). 'Access courses after ten years: A review', *Higher Education Quarterly*, **43**(2), 160–74.

Loder, C. (1991). 'Links between industry and higher education'. In J. Stevens and R. Mackay (eds) *Training and Competitiveness*, NEDO. London, Kogan Page.

Loder, C. (ed.) (1990). *Quality Assurance and Accountability in Higher Education*. London, Kogan Page.

Loder, C. (1992). 'A Survey of UK Social Science Research Resources'. London, ESRC/CHES.

Love, J. H. and McNicoll, I. H. (1990). 'The economic impact of university funding cuts', *Higher Education*, **19**(4), 481–95.

Massy, W. F. (1975). *Resource Management and Financial Equilibrium*. Washington, DC, National Association of College and University Business officers, Professional File Vol. 7, No. 7, pp. 1–7.

Mawditt, R. M. and Line, V. (1974). 'An investigation into the costing and management of university research grants and contracts. Program on institutional management in higher education'. Paper presented at the *General Meeting of Member Institutions of the Organisation for Economic Cooperation and Development, Paris (France)*. Paris, Centre for Educational Research and Innovation, Report No. IMHE-GC-74.44.

Moore, P. G. (1989). 'Marketing higher education', *Higher Education Quarterly*, **43**(2), 108–24.

Morgan, A. W. (1982). 'College and university planning in an era of contraction', *Higher Education*, **11**(5), 553–66.

Morris, A. (1974). 'Changing the ways of allocating resources to universities', *Higher Education Review*, **7**(1), 18–36.

Morris, A. (1975). 'Separate funding of university teaching and research', *Higher Education Review*, **7**(2), 42–58.

Morris, A. and Sizer, J. (ed.) (1982). *Resources and Higher Education*. Leverhulme Report No. 8. London, SRHE.

Navin, L. and Magura, M. (1976). 'A price index for university budgetary decisions', *Journal of Higher Education*, **48**(2), 216–25.

Neave, G. (1982). 'Cuts, constraints and vexations in European higher education', *Higher Education Review*, **15**(1), 5–19.

Neave, G. (1991). 'On visions of the market place', *Higher Education Quarterly*, **45**(1), 25–40.

Neuhoff, H. (1990). 'Private funding for university research in Europe: Some models and conceptions', *Higher Education Quarterly*, **44**(2), 163–73.

Norris, G. (ed.) (1974). University and polytechnic objectives, resource allocation and performance indices in the central services. Program on institutional management in higher education. Paper presented at the *General Conference of Member Institutions*. Paris, Organisation for Economic Cooperation and Development. Centre for Educational Research and Innovation. Report No. IMHE-GC-74.43.

O'Sullivan, M. and Dermot, A. (1986). 'UK scientists fret over slide in funding for university research', *Chemical and Engineering News*, **64**(11), 7–12.

Overseas Students Trust (1982). *A Policy for Overseas Students*. London, Overseas Students Trust.

Overseas Students Trust (1987). *The Next Steps: Overseas Policy into the 1990s*. London, OST.

Overseas Students Trust (1990). *Homes Far from Home: A Study of the Housing Needs and Expectations of Overseas Students in Britain*. London, OST.

Pollitt, C. (1990). 'Measuring university performance: Never mind the quality, never mind the width', *Higher Education Quarterly*, **44**(1), 60–81.

Port, J. and Burke, J. (1989). 'Business planning for higher education institutions', *Higher Education Quarterly*, **43**(2), 125–41.

Pratt, J. and Silverman, S. (1986). 'Responses to constraint in higher education: The 1984–85 NAB planning exercise in the English public sector', *International Journal of Institutional Management in Higher Education*, **10**(3), 208–18.

Pratt, J. and Silverman, S. (1989). *Responding to Constraint*. Milton Keynes, Open University Press.

Pratt, J. and Hillier, Y. (1991). *New Funding Mechanisms: Bidding for Funds in the PCFC Sector*. London, Centre for Higher Education Studies.

Quinn, T. F. J. (1978). 'A critical appraisal of modular courses and their relevance to the British System of higher education', *British Journal of Educational Technology*, **9**(1), 5–16.

Reid, I. *et al.* (1984). 'The cuts in British higher education: A Symposium', *British Journal of Sociology of Education*, **5**(2), 167–81.

Renton, T. (1985). *Government Policy on Overseas Students*. Mimeographed text of a speech made by Timothy Renton, MP Parliamentary Under-Secretary for Foreign and Commonwealth Affairs, 21 February.

Round Table (1989). 'Overseas Students: Private/Public Sector Interaction: Government and British Council Support'. Paper prepared for Round Table Meeting, October 1989 (mimeo).

Rowe, D. (1987). 'The university's role in assembling resources to establish and develop a Science Park', *International Journal of Institutional Management in Higher Education*, **11**(3), 303–10.

Rumble, G. W. S. V. (1976). 'The economics of the Open University of the United Kingdom'. Paper presented to the *Anglian Regional Management College/ Organization for Economic Cooperation and Development, 'International Management Development Programme for Senior Administrators in Institutions of Higher Education'*. Danbury, England, June 27–July 2.

Salter, B. (1983). 'Contract research: Universities and the knowledge market', *Higher Education Review*, **15**(2), 7–29.

Shattock, M. L. (1979). 'Retrenchment in US higher education: Some reflections on the resilience of the US and UK university systems', *Education Policy Bulletin*, **7**(2), 149–68.

Shattock, M. L. (1981a). *The Structure and Governance of Higher Education*. Leverhulme Report No. 9. London, SRHE.

Shattock, M. L. (1981b). 'University resource allocation procedures: Responses to change', *International Journal of Institutional Management in Higher Education*, **5**(3), 199–205.

Shattock, M. L. (1982). 'How should British universities plan for the 1980s?' *Higher Education*, **11**(2), 193–210.

Shattock, M. (1983). *Resource Allocation in British Universities*. SRHE Monograph 56. London, SRHE.

Shattock, M. L. *et al.* (1984). 'The British University Grants Committee 1919–83: Changing relationships with government and the universities', *Higher Education*, **13**(5), 471–99.

Shaw, K. E. (1978). 'Contraction and mergers of United Kingdom colleges on education: Some logistic comments', *Journal of Educational Administration*, **16**(2), 212–18.

Segal, N. (1985). *The Cambridge Phenomenon*. Cambridge, Segal Quince Wicksteed.

Siegel, B. N. (1966). *Towards a Theory of the Educational Firm*. Eugene, Oregon, Oregon University, Center for Advanced Study of Educational Administration. Report No. BR-5-0217.

Simpson, M. G. *et al.* (1972). *Planning University Development*. OECD Publications Center, Suite 1207, 1750 Pennsylvania Avenue, NW, Washington, DC 20006.

Simpson, W. A. (1985). 'Retrenchment in British Universities: Lessons learned', *Canadian Journal of Higher Education*, **15**(3), 73–91.

Sizer, J. (1987). 'British Universities' responses to financial reductions', *International Journal of Institutional Management in Higher Education*, **11**(3), 248–66.

Sizer, J. (1987). 'The impacts of financial reductions in British universities: 1981–84', *Higher Education*, **16**(5), 557–80.

Sizer, J. (1989). 'A critical examination of the events leading up to the UGC's grants letters dated 1st July 1981', *Higher Education*, **18**(6), 639–80.

Steedman, H. (1982). 'Recent developments in higher education in the United Kingdom', *European Journal of Education*, **17**(2), 193–203.

Taylor, B. J. R. (1981). 'Resource allocation in UK universities', *Journal of Tertiary Educational Administration*, **3**(1), 23–34.

Taylor, B. J. R. (1982a). 'Resource allocation in UK universities', *Association for Institutional Research, AIR Professional File*, Spring (1), 11.

Taylor, B. J. R. (1982b). 'The University of Bath in a national context', *Journal of Tertiary Educational Administration*, **4**(2), 155–66.

Taylor, J. (1987). 'Performance indicators in higher education: Recent developments in UK universities', *Australian Universities' Review*, **30**(2), 28–31.

Thompson, J. H. (1985). 'Issues requiring closer institutional government cooperation', *International Journal of Institutional Management in Higher Education*, **9**(1), 21–7.

Toyne, P. (1985). 'Mission and strategy: A case study of North East London Polytechnic', *International Journal of Institutional Management in Higher Education*, **9**(3), 323–8.

Training Agency (1989). 'Enterprise in higher education: Key features of the enterprise in higher education proposals', Training Agency, Sheffield.

Tribe, K. (1990). 'The accumulation of cultural capital: The funding of UK higher education in the twentieth century', *Higher Education Quarterly*, **44**(1), 21–34.

Turner, J. D. (1990). 'Universities, government policy and the study of education in Britain', *Journal of Education for Teaching*, **16**(1), 73–82.

Turner, D. and Platt, J. (1990). 'Bidding for funds in higher education', *Higher Education Review*, **22**(3), 19–33.

Turney, J. (1989). 'New models for matrix management', *Times Higher Education Supplement*, 24 March.

Walford, G. (1984). 'Note: The numbering of postgraduate research', *Higher Education Review*, **16**(2), 61–5.

Wagner, L. (ed.) (1982). *Agenda for Institutional Change in Higher Education*. Leverhulme Programme of Study into the Future of Higher Education, 3. Research into Higher Education Monographs, 45. London, SRHE.

Walker, R. and Stringer, P. (1991). 'Issues in the management of social science research centres', *Higher Education Quarterly*, **45**(1), 62–77.

Walker, A. and Wright, G. A. (1990). 'The funding of higher education in the UK: A contribution to the debate', *Higher Education Quarterly*, **44**(3), 230–44.

Walker, D. (1986). 'Universities in Britain agree to tenure changes to get bigger grants', *Chronicle of Higher Education*, **33**(13), 1–32.

Wasser, H. (1990). 'Changes in the European university: From traditional to entrepreneurial', *Higher Education Quarterly*, **44**(2), 110–22.

White, J. N. and Burnett, C. W. (eds) (1981). *Higher Education Literature: An Annotated Bibliography*. Phoenix, AZ, 85004, The Oryx Press.

Williams, B. (1991). *The Effects of the New Funding Mechanisms in Universities*. London, Centre for Higher Education Studies.

Williams, G. (1978). 'Reflections on a fading star', *Higher Education Review*, **11**(1), 15–25.

Williams, G. (1978). 'Higher education into the 1990s: A commentary and an examination of some policy options', *Higher Education Bulletin*, **6**(2), 17–47.

Williams, G. (1979). 'Educational planning past, present and future', *Education Policy Bulletin*, **7**(2), 125–40.

Williams, G. (1981). 'The main policy issues facing higher education in the 1980s and 1990s', *Education Policy Bulletin*, **9**(1), 13–38.

Williams, G. (1981). 'Of adversity and innovation in higher education', *Studies in Higher Education*, **6**(2), 131–8.

Williams, G. (1984). 'The SRHE–Leverhulme programme of study into the future of higher education in Britain', *Vestes*, **27**(1), 3–7.

Williams, G. (1987). 'Changing patterns of educational finance and the anticipated effects of institutional behaviour and educational outcomes'. In H. Thomas and T. Simkins (eds) *Economics and the Management of Education: Emerging Themes*. London, Falmer.

Williams, G. (1988). 'The debate about funding mechanisms', *Oxford Review of Education*, **1**, 59–68.

Williams, G. (1989). 'Prospects for higher education finance'. In C. Ball and H. Eggins (eds) *Higher Education into the 1990s: New Dimensions*. Milton Keynes, Open University Press.

Williams, G. and Blackstone, T. (1981). *Response to Adversity*. Leverhulme Report No. 10. London, SRHE.

Williams, G. (1990). *Financing Higher Education: Current Patterns*. Paris, OECD.

Williams, G. and Gordon, A. (1981). 'Perceived earnings functions and ex ante rates of return to post compulsory education in England', *Higher Education*, **10**(2), 199–227.

Williams, G. and Loder, C. (1990). 'Industry contributions to higher education funding and their effects'. In P. Wright (ed.) *Industry and Higher Education: Collaboration to Improve Students' Learning and Training*. Milton Keynes, SRHE/ Open University Press.

Williams, G. and Loder, C. (1991). 'Ménage à trois', *Times Higher Education Supplement*, 28 June.

Williams, G. and Loder, C. (1992). *When Worlds Collide: Business Funding of Higher Education*. London, Centre for Higher Education Studies, Institute of Education.

Williams, G., Woodhall, M. and O'Brien, U. (1986). *Overseas Students and Their Place of Study: A Report of a Survey*. London, Overseas Students Trust.

Williams, G., Metcalfe, D. and Blackstone, T. (1974). *The Academic Labour Market*. Amsterdam, Elsevier.

Williams, P. (ed.) (1981). *The Overseas Student Question: Studies for a Policy*. London, Heinemann for the Overseas Students Trust.

Woodhall, M. (1989). 'Marketing British higher education overseas: The response to the introduction of full-cost fees', *Higher Education Quarterly*, **43**(2), 142–59.

Yorke, D. M. (1987). 'Indicators of institutional achievement: Some theoretical and empirical considerations', *Higher Education*, **16**(1), 3–20.

Ziman, J. (1991). 'Academic Science as a System of Markets', *Higher Education Quarterly*, **45**(1), 41–61.

Index

The Society for Research into Higher Education

The Society for Research into Higher Education exists both to stimulate and co-ordinate research into all aspects of higher education. It aims to improve the quality of higher education through the encouragement of debate and publication on issues of policy, on the organization and management of higher education institutions, and on the curriculum and teaching methods.

The Society's income is derived from subscriptions, sales of its books and journals, conference fees and grants. It receives no subsidies and is wholly independent. Its individual members include teachers, researchers, managers and students. Its corporate members are institutions of higher education, research institutes,professional, industrial and governmental bodies. Members are not only from the UK, but from elsewhere in Europe, from America, Canada and Australasia, and it regards its international work as amongst its most important activities.

Under the imprint SRHE & Open University Press, the Society is a specialist publisher of research, having some 30 titles in print. The Editorial Board of the Society's Imprint seeks authoritative research or study in the field. It offers competitive royalties, a highly recognizable format in both hard- and paper-back and the world-wide reputation of the Open University Press.

The Society also publishes *Studies in Higher Education* (three times a year), which is mainly concerned with academic issues, *Higher Education Quarterly* (formerly *Universities Quarterly*), mainly concerned with policy issues. *Abstracts* (three times a year), and SRHE NEWS (four times a year).

The Society holds a major annual conference in December, jointly with an institution of higher education. In 1991, the topic was 'Research and Higher Education in Europe', with the University of Leicester. Future conferences include in 1992, 'Learning to Effect', with Nottingham Polytechnic, and in 1993, 'Governments and the Higher Education Curriculum' with the University of Sussex. In addition it holds regular seminars and consultations on topics of current interest.

The Society's committees, study groups and branches are run by members. The groups at present include:
Teacher Education Study Group
Continuing Education Group
Staff Development Group
Excellence in Teaching & Learning
Women in Higher Education Group.

Benefits to members
Individual

Individual members receive:

- The NEWS, the Society's publications list, conference details and other material included in mailings.
- Reduced rates for *Studies in Higher Education* (£9.75 per year – full price £72) and *Higher Education Quarterly* (£12.35 per year – full price £43).
- A 35% discount on all Open University Press & SRHE publications.
- Free copies of the Proceedings (or Precedings) – commissioned papers on the theme of the Annual Conference.
- Free copies of *Higher Education Abstracts*.
- Reduced rates for conferences.
- Extensive contacts and scope for facilitating initiatives.
- Reduced reciprocal memberships.

Corporate

Corporate members receive:

- All benefits of individual members, plus
- Free copies of *Studies in Higher Education*.
- Unlimited copies of the Society's publications at reduced rates.
- Special rates for its members, e.g. to the Annual Conference.

Subscriptions August 1991–July 1992
Individual members

standard fee	£ 47
hardship (e.g. unwaged)	£ 22
students and retired	£ 14

Corporate members

a) teaching institutions	
under 1000 students	£170
up to 3000 students	£215
over 3000 students	£320
b) non-teaching institutions	up to £325
c) industrial/professional bodies	up to £325

Further information: SRHE, 344–354 Gray's Inn Road, London, WC1X 8BP, UK. Tel: 071 837 7880
Catalogue: SRHE & Open University Press, Celtic Court, 22 Ballmoor, Buckingham MK18 1XW. Tel: (0280) 823388